Eyewitness
CLIMATE
CHANGE

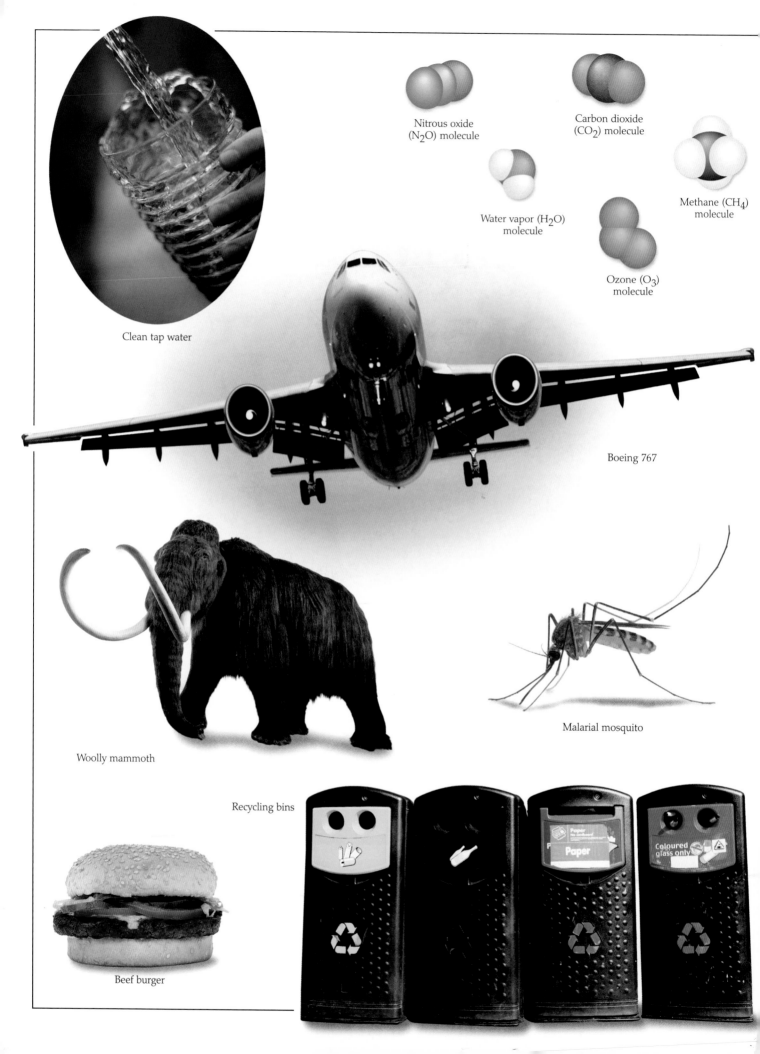

Nitrous oxide
(N$_2$O) molecule

Carbon dioxide
(CO$_2$) molecule

Water vapor (H$_2$O)
molecule

Methane (CH$_4$)
molecule

Ozone (O$_3$)
molecule

Clean tap water

Boeing 767

Woolly mammoth

Malarial mosquito

Recycling bins

Beef burger

Eyewitness
CLIMATE CHANGE

Written by
JOHN WOODWARD

Satellite infrared image of Earth's
temperature at night

DK Publishing

Vegetable pizza

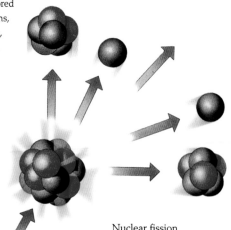

Offshore wind farm

DK

LONDON, NEW YORK,
MELBOURNE, MUNICH, AND DELHI

Consultant Dr Piers Forster

Project editor Margaret Hynes
Managing editor Camilla Hallinan
Managing art editor Owen Peyton Jones
Art director Martin Wilson
Publishing manager Sunita Gahir
Category publisher Andrea Pinnington
Picture researcher Sarah & Roland Smithies
DK picture library Lucy Claxton, Rose Horridge,
Myriam Megharbi, Emma Shepherd, Romaine Werblow
Production editor Hitesh Patel
Senior production controller Man Fai Lau
Jacket designer Andy Smith

DK DELHI
Art Director Shefali Upadhyay
Designers Govind Mittal, Tannishtha Chakraborti
DTP Designer Harish Aggarwal

This Eyewitness ® Book has been conceived by
Dorling Kindersley Limited and Editions Gallimard.

First published in the United States in 2008
by DK Publishing, 375 Hudson Street, New York, New York 10014

08 09 10 11 12 10 9 8 7 6 5 4 3 2 1
ED619 – 01/08

A catalog record for this book
is available from the Library of Congress.

ISBN: 978-0-7566-4194-8

Colour reproduction by Colourscan, Singapore
Printed and bound by Leo Paper Products Ltd, China

Discover more at
www.dk.com

Layers of Earth's
atmosphere

Gasoline pump, US

Desert, Israel

Nuclear fission
reaction

Contents

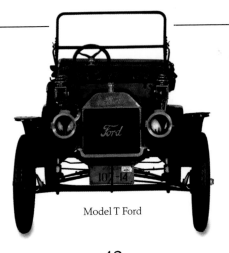

Model T Ford

6
Earth's climate
8
The greenhouse effect
10
The carbon cycle
12
Checks and balances
14
Natural climate change
16
The human impact
18
Burning the forests
20
Fosil fuels
22
Our carbon culture
24
Adding to the problem
26
Heatwaves and droughts
28
Melting ice
30
Warming oceans
32
Oceanic research
34
Living with the heat
36
Plight of the polar bear
38
Predicting future climates
40
The next century

42
What scares the scientists?
44
Climate change and society
46
Adapting to climate change
48
Combating climate change
50
Cutting the carbon
52
Nuclear power
54
Renewable energy
56
Power for the people
58
Energy efficiency
60
Green transportation
62
Your carbon footprint
64
Greenhouse gas producers
66
Timeline
69
Find out more
70
Glossary
72
Index

Earth's Climate

EARTH IS A UNIQUE PLANET. It is the only one in the Solar System that has both an atmosphere and oceans of water, and these have created ideal conditions for life to evolve and flourish. Currents in the atmosphere and oceans carry heat and moisture around the globe, so life can exist almost everywhere. These currents also create the weather. This changes daily, but in predictable patterns. The pattern of weather in a particular place is its climate. Climates vary slowly over time, forcing life to adapt to new conditions, but recently the rate of climate change has sped up.

LIVING PLANET
Our planet is a small oasis of life in the vastness of space. There may be others in the universe, but this is the only one we know about. Earth is close enough to the Sun to stop the oceans from freezing solid. A force of attraction called gravity holds on to the planet's atmosphere, and this provides living things with vital gases. It also acts like an insulating blanket, keeping temperatures within the limits that allow life to survive.

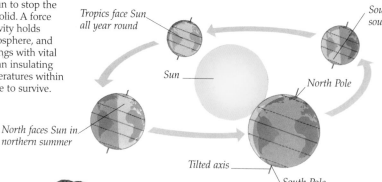

Tropics face Sun all year round

South faces Sun in southern summer

Sun

North Pole

North faces Sun in northern summer

Tilted axis

South Pole

TILTED EARTH
The Sun shines directly on the tropics around the Equator, with a concentrated energy that creates tropical climates. Sunlight strikes the poles at an angle, dispersing its energy and allowing ice sheets to form. The spinning Earth is tilted on its axis, so as it orbits the Sun, the Sun's rays heat the north more intensely during the northern summer, and the south more intensely during the northern winter. It takes a year for Earth to orbit the Sun, creating annual seasons.

BARREN DESERT
Liquid water is vital to living things, so regions where any water is either permanently frozen or is dried up by the Sun are lifeless deserts. Plants may be able to grow in places where there are reserves of liquid water below the surface, but much of the landscape is bare rock and sand. In a hot desert like this one in Israel, a slight rise in average temperature could wipe out all traces of life.

TEEMING WITH LIFE
In regions where the climate is warm and wet, living things can grow and multiply to form rich ecosystems like this rainforest. A tangle of trees and other plants provide food for a huge variety of insects and other animals. Yet they have all evolved to flourish in the conditions created by a particular type of climate, and many may not be able to survive rapid climate change.

SWIRLING CURRENTS

Intense sunlight in the tropics generates warm air currents that flow toward the poles in a series of rising and sinking "cells," transferring heat to areas where solar heating is less intense. This cools the tropics and warms the temperate and polar regions, giving the planet a more even climate. Winds and weather systems driven by high-level air currents also carry moisture from the oceans over the continents, where it falls as rain or snow. This provides the vital water that allows life to flourish on land, from the Equator to the fringes of the polar ice. Variations in temperature and rainfall create a variety of climate zones such as deserts and rainforests, which can be recognized by both their climates and their wildlife.

CHANGING CLIMATES

For most of human history, the world's climates have been unusually stable, enabling civilizations to rise and prosper. But climates are changing. Polar ice is melting, temperate regions are suffering more heatwaves and severe storms, and the tropics seem to be getting drier. Climate scientists working at research stations like this one in Antarctica are certain that the world is getting warmer.

Earth's spin makes temperate winds swerve east

Sinking dry air creates deserts

High-level jet streams blow east

Atmospheric cell

Rising warm, moist air near the Equator causes rain over the tropics

Earth spins toward the east

Moving weather systems transfer water from the oceans to the continents

Earth's spin makes tropical winds swerve west

WARMING WORLD

Global average temperatures started rising in about 1900. They have risen and fallen many times since then, but the trend has crept upward—slowly at first, but more rapidly since the 1970s. The rise in temperature roughly matches the rise of modern industry, the growth of huge cities, and the increasing quantities of fuel such as coal and oil that we burn to provide energy for heating, electrical power, and transportation.

SVANTE ARRHENIUS

In the 1890s Swedish chemist Svante Arrhenius decided that past ice ages might have been caused by fewer volcanic eruptions pumping gases such as carbon dioxide into the atmosphere. These gases retain heat, so reducing them would make Earth cool down. He then wondered what would happen if intense industrial activity produced more of these gases by burning fuels such as coal. He realized that it would make the world warm up—and so discovered the factor that linked industrialization and fuel use with changing global temperatures. He was not to know that, within a century, this process would start to have a dramatic effect on world climate.

The Greenhouse Effect

Earth would be a lifeless ball of rock if it did not have an atmosphere. This is partly because living things rely on the atmosphere to supply them with essential elements such as carbon, nitrogen, and oxygen. Living things also depend on the atmosphere to maintain the temperature that they need to survive. The layers of air that surround the planet act as both sunscreen and insulation, shielding life from the fiercest of the Sun's rays while retaining heat that would otherwise escape back into space at night. This feature of the atmosphere is known as the greenhouse effect. Life on Earth would be impossible without it, but its increasing power is also causing global warming.

RETAINING THE HEAT
A lot of shortwave solar radiation, or sunlight, passes straight through the atmosphere and reaches Earth's surface. As Earth absorbs this solar energy it warms up, and radiates heat in the form of invisible, longwave infrared radiation. This does not pass straight through the atmosphere. Instead, much of its energy is absorbed by gases in the air. As these gases absorb energy, they warm up. Like Earth's surface, they radiate some of this heat back into space, but they also radiate some back to Earth, keeping the planet's surface warmer than it would otherwise be. This is the greenhouse effect. The gases that cause it are known as greenhouse gases.

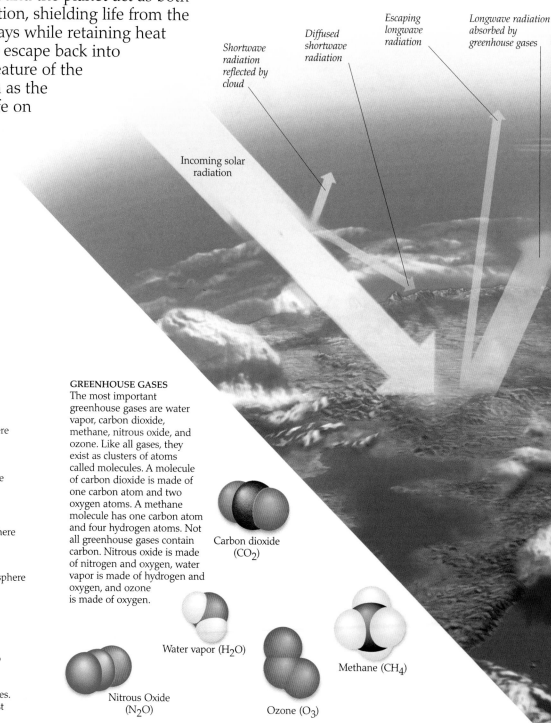

Shortwave radiation reflected by cloud

Diffused shortwave radiation

Escaping longwave radiation

Longwave radiation absorbed by greenhouse gases

Incoming solar radiation

Exosphere

Thermosphere

Mesosphere

Stratosphere

Troposphere

GREENHOUSE GASES
The most important greenhouse gases are water vapor, carbon dioxide, methane, nitrous oxide, and ozone. Like all gases, they exist as clusters of atoms called molecules. A molecule of carbon dioxide is made of one carbon atom and two oxygen atoms. A methane molecule has one carbon atom and four hydrogen atoms. Not all greenhouse gases contain carbon. Nitrous oxide is made of nitrogen and oxygen, water vapor is made of hydrogen and oxygen, and ozone is made of oxygen.

Carbon dioxide (CO_2)

Water vapor (H_2O)

Methane (CH_4)

Nitrous Oxide (N_2O)

Ozone (O_3)

EARTH'S ATMOSPHERE
The atmosphere is mainly made up of nitrogen and oxygen gas, plus much smaller amounts of carbon dioxide, water vapor, and other gases. It forms a series of layers, with most of the gases concentrated in the lowest layer, the troposphere.

LIFE SUPPORT

If this rose continues to endure freezing temperatures, it will freeze solid and die. The same thing would happen to all living things if Earth were stripped of its atmosphere overnight. Daytime temperatures would be scorching, but nighttime temperatures would plummet to far below freezing. The average global temperature would sink from 57°F (14°C) to about 0°F (–18°C). Without the greenhouse effect, life on Earth could not have evolved.

Heat escapes into space

Warm gases heat Earth's surface

Greenhouse gases in the atmosphere

COLD NEIGHBOR

The Moon is a lot smaller than Earth, and much lighter. Because of its low mass, it does not have as much gravity, so any gas that might seep from its interior just drifts off into space instead of forming an atmosphere. As there is no atmosphere, there can be no greenhouse effect to retain the heat of the Sun, so although the Moon is the same distance from the Sun as we are, its average surface temperature is much lower. This is one reason why there is no life on the Moon.

Volcanoes on Venus

GREENHOUSE PLANET

Venus is the same size as Earth, and has an atmosphere, but it is too close to the Sun for oceans to form. On Earth the oceans absorb carbon dioxide from the air, reducing the greenhouse effect. But on Venus there are no oceans, so all the carbon dioxide erupted by the planet's volcanoes has stayed in its atmosphere. The result is a hugely powerful greenhouse effect that raises the surface temperature of Venus to above 930°F (500°C)—hot enough to melt lead.

CHARLES KEELING

Of the main atmospheric greenhouse gases, carbon dioxide is one of the most important. It absorbs a lot less energy per molecule than other greenhouse gases such as nitrous oxide and methane, but there is much more of it. Measurements of carbon dioxide in the air by US scientist Charles Keeling show that its concentration has been increasing every year since 1958.

Balloon holds carbon dioxide sample

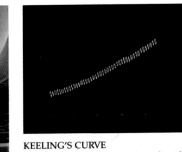

KEELING'S CURVE

Keeling's atmospheric carbon dioxide measurements create a rising zigzag line on a graph. The zigzag effect indicates an annual rise and fall—the fall is caused by absorption of carbon dioxide by plants growing on the vast northern continents in summer. But the trend of the graph keeps rising, from 315 parts of carbon dioxide per million of air in 1958 to 380 today.

The Carbon Cycle

CARBON EXISTS IN PURE FORM as graphite—the "lead" in a pencil, for example—and diamonds. Yet if it combines with oxygen, it forms carbon dioxide gas, and with hydrogen it forms methane. Green plants use carbon dioxide to make food. They absorb it from the air, and use the Sun's energy to combine it with water to make a carbohydrate, sugar. Sugar stores energy, and if it is combined with oxygen, the energy is released to fuel life processes. This reaction also turns the sugar back into water and carbon dioxide, which pass back into the atmosphere. Carbon dioxide is also released through burning and decay, absorbed and released by ocean water, locked up in limestones that form on shallow sea floors, and erupted from volcanoes. So carbon is always passing between living things, the atmosphere, oceans, and rocks, in an exchange called the carbon cycle.

Plant matter

Peat

Lignite (soft coal)

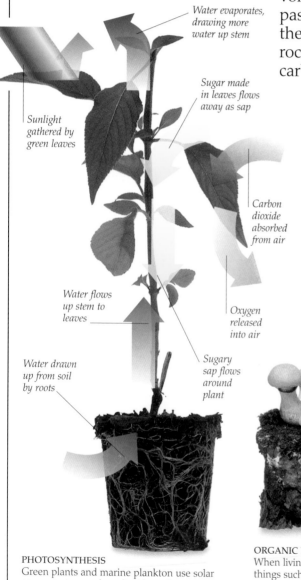

Water evaporates, drawing more water up stem

Sugar made in leaves flows away as sap

Sunlight gathered by green leaves

Carbon dioxide absorbed from air

Water flows up stem to leaves

Oxygen released into air

Water drawn up from soil by roots

Sugary sap flows around plant

RESPIRATION
Plants and animals use oxygen to release the energy stored in sugar and other carbohydrates. Known as respiration, this turns the sugar back into carbon dioxide and water. Animals breathe in the oxygen, and breathe out to lose carbon dioxide and water vapor, which is often visible on a cold day.

CARBON STORAGE
When a plant or animal dies, it usually starts decaying right away, and its carbon content soon returns to the air. But sometimes it is buried in such a way that it does not decay properly. Dead plants that sink into a waterlogged bog often do not rot away, but turn into deep layers of peat. Eventually the peat may be compressed into coal, a process that stores the carbon for millions of years instead of for the lifetime of the plants.

Coal

ORGANIC DECAY
When living things die, other living things such as these fungi and bacteria start recycling their basic ingredients. This process of decay often combines the carbon in the dead tissues with oxygen, so it returns to the atmosphere as carbon dioxide. Another type of decay combines the carbon with hydrogen to form methane.

PHOTOSYNTHESIS
Green plants and marine plankton use solar energy to turn carbon dioxide and water into sugar. This process, which is called photosynthesis, also releases oxygen. Sugar stores the energy of the Sun in chemical form, and nearly all living things on Earth rely on this energy to build their tissues and fuel their activities. Life is built on carbon.

Anthracite (hard coal)

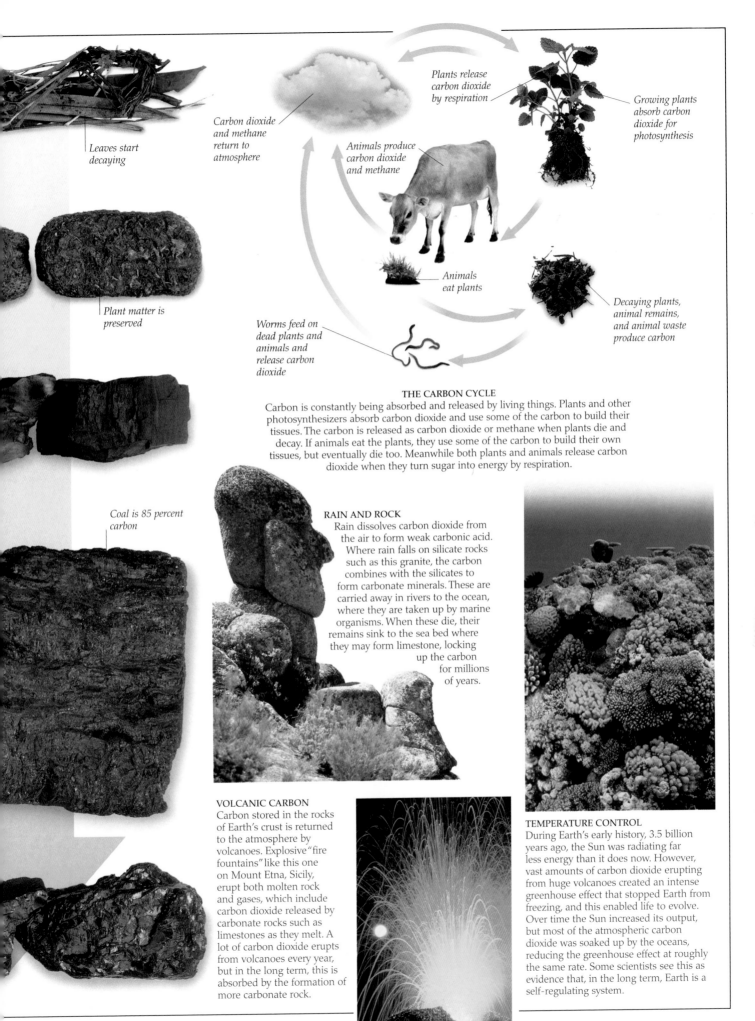

Leaves start
decaying

Plant matter is
preserved

Coal is 85 percent
carbon

Carbon dioxide
and methane
return to
atmosphere

Plants release
carbon dioxide
by respiration

Growing plants
absorb carbon
dioxide for
photosynthesis

Animals produce
carbon dioxide
and methane

Animals
eat plants

Decaying plants,
animal remains,
and animal waste
produce carbon

Worms feed on
dead plants and
animals and
release carbon
dioxide

THE CARBON CYCLE

Carbon is constantly being absorbed and released by living things. Plants and other photosynthesizers absorb carbon dioxide and use some of the carbon to build their tissues. The carbon is released as carbon dioxide or methane when plants die and decay. If animals eat the plants, they use some of the carbon to build their own tissues, but eventually die too. Meanwhile both plants and animals release carbon dioxide when they turn sugar into energy by respiration.

RAIN AND ROCK

Rain dissolves carbon dioxide from the air to form weak carbonic acid. Where rain falls on silicate rocks such as this granite, the carbon combines with the silicates to form carbonate minerals. These are carried away in rivers to the ocean, where they are taken up by marine organisms. When these die, their remains sink to the sea bed where they may form limestone, locking up the carbon for millions of years.

TEMPERATURE CONTROL

During Earth's early history, 3.5 billion years ago, the Sun was radiating far less energy than it does now. However, vast amounts of carbon dioxide erupting from huge volcanoes created an intense greenhouse effect that stopped Earth from freezing, and this enabled life to evolve. Over time the Sun increased its output, but most of the atmospheric carbon dioxide was soaked up by the oceans, reducing the greenhouse effect at roughly the same rate. Some scientists see this as evidence that, in the long term, Earth is a self-regulating system.

VOLCANIC CARBON

Carbon stored in the rocks of Earth's crust is returned to the atmosphere by volcanoes. Explosive "fire fountains" like this one on Mount Etna, Sicily, erupt both molten rock and gases, which include carbon dioxide released by carbonate rocks such as limestones as they melt. A lot of carbon dioxide erupts from volcanoes every year, but in the long term, this is absorbed by the formation of more carbonate rock.

Checks and Balances

THE ENERGY THAT EARTH soaks up
from the Sun is more or less balanced by
the energy that it radiates out into space, but
only in the long term. Short-term imbalances
can make the planet colder or warmer.
These temperature changes can lead to mass
extinctions, like the one that wiped out the
dinosaurs 65 million years ago. Once the
balance is upset, this can lead to other changes
in Earth's climate system, which are called
feedbacks. There are two types of feedback.
Negative feedbacks resist temperature change
by reducing the effects of the initial imbalance.
Positive feedbacks enhance the initial imbalance,
leading to a greater temperature change.
Scientists are concerned that steadily rising
global temperatures may trigger powerful
positive feedbacks that make Earth a lot
warmer in the coming decades, with serious
consequences for us all.

NEGATIVE FEEDBACKS
Some natural processes resist change. When intense sunlight warms the
ocean surface, water evaporates and rises into the air as invisible water vapor.
As it rises it cools and forms clouds, which shade the ocean so it cools down.
Eventually evaporation and cloud formation stops, so sunlight can warm the
ocean again. This is an example of
negative feedback.

POSITIVE FEEDBACKS
When ice forms or snow
falls, the dazzling white
surface acts like a mirror.
It reflects solar energy,
so less heat is absorbed
by the ground and more
ice forms. This is called
the albedo effect. It is an
example of positive feedback,
which promotes change rather
than resisting it.

SOLAR ENERGY
When sunlight strikes Earth's atmosphere, about
a third of its energy—shown here in watts per
square foot—is returned to space by reflection
from clouds, from tiny airborne particles called
aerosols, and from the Earth's surface. More
is absorbed by the atmosphere, leaving
less than half to be absorbed by
the sea and land. These warm up
and radiate heat energy back
into the atmosphere, where
some is absorbed by
greenhouse gases.

107 — *Reflected solar radiation*

342 — *Incoming solar radiation*

67 — *Absorbed by the atmosphere*

77 — *Reflected by the clouds, aerosols, and atmosphere*

Reflected by the surface — 30

Absorbed by the surface — 168

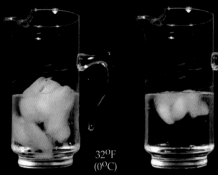

14°F
(−10°C)

23°F
(−5°C)

30°F
(−1°C)

32°F
(0°C)

34°F
(1°C)

TIPPING POINTS

Steady change can have sudden, dramatic effects. If a jug full of ice cubes is warmed up from 14°F (−10°C) at the rate of a degree or two an hour, nothing at all happens until the temperature rises to just above 32°F (0°C). Then all the ice cubes start melting. Climate scientists worry that rising global temperatures may pass similar tipping points, causing sudden changes and triggering positive feedbacks that accelerate the process.

JAMES LOVELOCK

British scientist James Lovelock is famous for his theory that living things regulate the climate and the chemistry of the atmosphere in their own interest. Over the long term, a web of negative feedbacks ensures that life survives, despite catastrophes that cause mass extinctions. The theory is named after Gaia, the Greek goddess of the Earth.

CARBON UPTAKE

One of the main checks on the greenhouse effect involves plants and marine plankton, as the more carbon dioxide there is, the faster they grow and the more they absorb. Here plants are being grown in a sealed enclosure containing extra carbon dioxide to see how they respond.

235 — Outgoing longwave radiation

Emitted by clouds

165 — Radiated by greenhouse gases

30

40 — Transmitted through the atmosphere

350 — Absorbed by greenhouse gases

Radiated by greenhouse gases

324 — Absorbed by the surface

Radiated from surface

324

390

Natural Climate Change

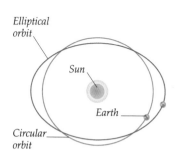

Elliptical orbit
Sun
Earth
Circular orbit

ORBITAL CYCLES
Earth's climate changes in regular cycles caused by variations in its orbit around the Sun. These are known as Milankovitch cycles, after the Serbian mathematician who calculated them. One 100,000-year cycle changes the planet's orbit from almost circular to elliptical, affecting its annual temperature range.

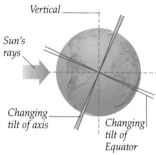

Vertical
Sun's rays
Changing tilt of axis
Changing tilt of Equator

TILTED EARTH
Every 24 hours, Earth spins around an axis that is currently tilted at 23.5° from vertical. The spin gives us night and day, while the tilt causes our winters and summers. But the tilt varies over a 42,000-year cycle, from 21.6° to 24.5°. This alters the way sunlight strikes the surface of the planet, changing the areas of the tropical and polar regions and affecting global air circulation.

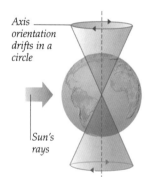

Axis orientation drifts in a circle
Sun's rays

AXIS DRIFT
Another cycle alters the orientation of Earth's axis, so it is aligned with different points in space. Currently the North Pole points to the pole star, Polaris, but over time it drifts away to point at other stars, returning after 25,800 years. This changes the dates of the seasons, so halfway through the cycle, the dates of winter and summer are reversed.

CLIMATE SCIENTISTS AGREE that the current rise in average global temperature is being caused by human activities. But climate change has occurred in the past, before people started changing the world, and indeed before humans existed. These shifts were caused by natural cycles that affect Earth's orbit around the Sun, by changes in solar radiation levels, and by catastrophic natural events such as massive volcanic eruptions. Some of these changes seem to have triggered positive feedbacks that dramatically increased their effect. It is possible that this might happen again.

Sunspot

Woolly mammoth

ICE AGES
Earth has passed through several ice ages that were caused at least partly by orbital cycles. We are now living in a warm phase of an ice age that peaked about 20,000 years ago. Ice sheets covered vast areas of the north, fringed by snowy tundra that was the home of cold-adapted animals like this woolly mammoth.

SUNSPOTS AND PLAGES
The Sun has bursts of activity that cause dark patches, called sunspots, to appear on its surface within lighter areas called plages. The more sunspots and plages there are, the more energy the Sun is radiating. There are more of them now than in the early 1800s, but the variations in solar energy that they cause are quite small, and they do not match the current pattern of climate change.

GEOLOGICAL EVIDENCE
Clues to the climates of the distant past can be found in the rocks. Some exposed rocks in the Sahara show scratches made by moving ice some 480 million years ago, and thick layers of red sandstone in northern Europe were once sand dunes that built up in scorchingly hot deserts. The thick white chalk rock at the top of this English cliff was formed in a shallow tropical sea during the age of the dinosaurs.

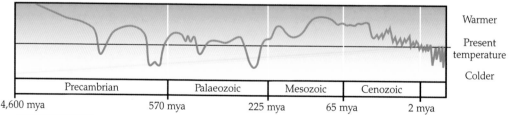

Warmer
Present temperature
Colder

| Precambrian | Palaeozoic | Mesozoic | Cenozoic | |
4,600 mya   570 mya   225 mya   65 mya   2 mya

THE LONG VIEW
Evidence from rocks, fossils, and other sources shows how Earth's average temperature has changed since it formed 4,600 million years ago (mya). During most of geological time, it has been warmer than it is now, but with ice ages during the Precambrian and Palaeozoic eras. The Mesozoic age of dinosaurs was a warm period, but temperatures fell during the Cenozoic era until they reached the coldest phases of the current ice age.

CONTINENTAL DRIFT
Over millions of years, the shifting plates of the Earth's crust move the continents into new arrangements, changing their climates. Some 250 million years ago, this process had created the "supercontinent" of Pangaea, which had a very dry desert climate because most of it was so far from the ocean.

DINOSAUR SUMMER
When dinosaurs roamed during the Mesozoic era of 250 to 65 million years ago, the world had a mainly warm climate. Near the end of the era, the average global temperature was 9°F (5°C) higher than today.

VOLCANIC ERUPTIONS
Some volcanic eruptions can propel dust and gas into the stratosphere. The gases include carbon dioxide, water vapor, and sulfur dioxide. The water and sulfur form droplets of sulfuric acid that can drift in the stratosphere for years, obscuring the Sun and causing global cooling of 1.8°F (1°C) or more. But the carbon dioxide stays in the atmosphere for over a century, causing global warming. Massive eruptions in the past may have dramatically changed the climate, but recent eruptions like Mt. Pinatubo (left) have not been big enough.

THE LITTLE ICE AGE
From the 1300s to around 1850, the Northern Hemisphere suffered a "Little Ice Age," which reached its coldest point in the mid-1400s. In Europe harvests failed and people starved. The bitterly cold winters created the frozen landscapes portrayed in many paintings of the period, such as this one painted by Dutch artist Hendrick Avercamp in the early 1600s. The cause of the Little Ice Age is still not known, but it may have been related to volcanic activity.

The Human Impact

THE LAST CENTURY HAS SEEN an average global air temperature rise of nearly 1.4°F (0.8°C), measured at ground level. This may not seem like much, but the world has warmed by only 7°F (4°C) in the 200 centuries since the peak of the last ice age, so this recent rise indicates a sharp upturn in the rate of warming. At the same time, we have enjoyed a technological revolution that has changed our lives, but this has been made possible only by massive consumption of energy. Most of this energy has been generated using fuel that, when burned, releases carbon dioxide. This has increased the concentration of carbon dioxide in the air. The increase closely matches the rise in global air temperature, so it is very likely that accelerated global warming is being caused by our modern, energy-hungry way of life.

Green and yellow show the Sahara is cooler than the ocean

Tropical Atlantic is warmer than the land at night

The tops of tropical storm clouds are icy cold

Southern Africa is as hot as the tropical ocean

TAKING EARTH'S TEMPERATURE
All over the world, people make daily records of temperature. Remote sensors in space can also detect surface temperatures, as shown in this infrared view of Earth at night, which was made by a weather satellite. Local temperatures vary a lot through the year, but when all the information is collated to give an average global temperature, it shows that the world is getting warmer.

Climate scientists at an Antarctic research station

CLUES FROM THE PAST
Scientists can use various techniques to compare current temperatures and rates of change with those of the distant past. Some of the best evidence comes from ice cores—samples of ice removed from the Greenland and Antarctic ice sheets. These contain air bubbles trapped over the past 650,000 years. The atomic structure of the oxygen in these bubbles gives a measure of local air temperature over that time, and this may reflect global temperature changes.

Ice core is carefully slid out of the hollow drill

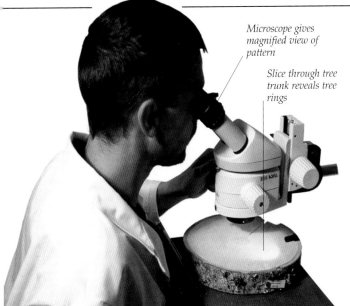

Microscope gives magnified view of pattern

Slice through tree trunk reveals tree rings

TREE RINGS

Every year a living tree adds a layer of new wood to the outside of its trunk. This new layer is thicker in a warm year and thinner in a cold one, forming a pattern of rings that records the sequence of warm and cold years. If one of these tree rings can be dated, the pattern gives a record of local climate for the life of the tree. In some cases this can be thousands of years. A similar technique is used to study growth rings in the corals that form in tropical seas.

Arctic ivory gull is threatened by loss of sea ice

THE PRIME SUSPECT

Air bubbles trapped in ice cores show that the level of carbon dioxide in the atmosphere in 1700 was roughly 280 parts carbon dioxide per million of air. Today, air samples taken by devices attached to the top of towers like this reveal that the level has now increased to 380 parts carbon dioxide. The 100 ppm increase in carbon dioxide in the atmosphere has added significantly to the greenhouse effect that keeps the planet warm, and this is one of the main reasons why global temperatures have risen and are continuing to rise.

AVERAGES AND EXTREMES

While the 1.4°F (0.8°C) temperature rise over one hundred years does not sound very serious, some animals, including this ivory gull, are in decline because of it. The figure is an average of all the temperature changes all over the world. In some places the temperature may not have risen at all. In others, such as in parts of the Arctic where the gull lives, local winter temperatures have risen by up to 7°F (4°C) since the 1950s, and the ice on which this bird finds its food has melted away.

GRAPHIC PROOF

Since 1900 the average global temperature has risen, as shown by the blue line on the graph. This cannot be due to natural causes alone, because if they are modeled by computers, the resulting temperature, (in green) does not rise in the same way. When human influences are added, the computer gives the temperature shown by the orange line. The close match shows that human factors such as the release of greenhouse gases are the main reason for global warming.

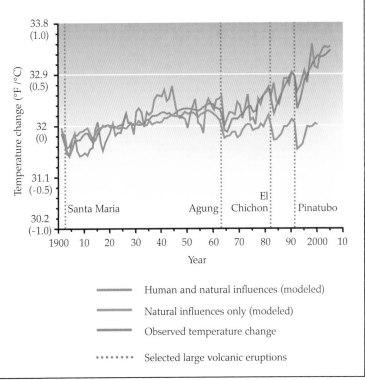

Temperature change (°F /°C)

33.8 (1.0)
32.9 (0.5)
32 (0)
31.1 (-0.5)
30.2 (-1.0)

Santa Maria   Agung   El Chichon   Pinatubo

1900 10 20 30 40 50 60 70 80 90 2000 10

Year

▬▬▬ Human and natural influences (modeled)

▬▬▬ Natural influences only (modeled)

▬▬▬ Observed temperature change

········· Selected large volcanic eruptions

Burning the Forests

CLIMATE CHANGE IS BEING CAUSED by a combination of factors, but the most important is the increase of greenhouse gases in the atmosphere, and especially carbon dioxide. Most of this extra carbon dioxide is being released by burning carbon-rich fuels. This is the same process that turns sugar into energy in our bodies, but it is more violent, releasing the energy as searing heat. The most basic of all fuels is wood, which people have been burning for thousands of years to keep warm and to cook their food. Huge increases in human populations have greatly increased the amount of wood that is burned like this each year. At the same time, vast forests are being cut down and burned to clear land for farming, ranching, and road building, especially in the tropics. This is also contributing to climate change by releasing all the carbon that the forest trees have absorbed over their lifetimes.

CARBON STORES
As a tree grows, it absorbs carbon dioxide and converts it into sugar, plant fiber, and wood. The wood stores carbon, but when the tree dies and decays, the carbon is released. In mature forests, dead trees are decaying as fast as live trees are growing. So although such forests act as carbon stores, they release as much carbon dioxide as they absorb.

Firestick used to burn forest

SLASH AND BURN
When trees catch fire, the carbon in their timber combines with oxygen to release energy and carbon dioxide. Wildfires are part of the natural carbon cycle, and the carbon dioxide they release is soon absorbed by young trees. But if a forest is cut down, burned, and not allowed to regrow, all its carbon is turned into carbon dioxide that increases the greenhouse effect.

CHANGE OF LAND USE
If a burned forest is able to regrow, the new trees eventually soak up the carbon dioxide released by the fire. But this may take a century or more, because young trees do not absorb as much carbon dioxide as big, mature trees. If the land is planted with crops like these, or becomes grassland, the small plants absorb even less carbon dioxide—and when they are harvested or grazed by animals, the carbon they contain is released again.

TROPICAL DESTRUCTION
Huge areas of tropical forest are being destroyed. Brazil has lost more than 163,000 sq miles (423,000 sq km) of forest since 1990—enough to cover California—and Indonesia has lost nearly 116,000 sq miles (300,000 sq km). In the Caribbean state of Haiti, more than 95 percent of the forests have been cut down, devastating the landscape. This photograph shows the border between Haiti, on the left, and the neighboring Dominican Republic which still has large tracts of forest.

STRIPPED SOIL

When forests are cut
down, the bare ground often
reflects more sunlight than the trees that have been
removed, causing cooling. But meanwhile the exposed
soils start releasing greenhouse gases such as carbon
dioxide, nitrous oxide, and methane. In Indonesia,
the soils of swampy lowland forests contain a lot
of waterlogged peat. If the forest is cut down,
the peat can dry out and decay. As shown
in this photograph, the peat sometimes
burns, releasing more carbon dioxide.
Altogether, the greenhouse gases
released by deforestation far
outweigh the cooling effect
of the bare ground.

*Huge smoke
cloud hangs
over Borneo*

SMOKE AND SOOT

Forest fires generated the smoke seen here in the atmosphere
above Borneo in 2002. The smoke is made up of gases and
soot that combine with water vapor to form clouds of airborne
particles called aerosols. These can absorb and reflect sunlight,
causing cooling. But carbon dioxide released at the same time
persists for much longer, adding to the greenhouse effect.

SUSTAINABLE FUEL

Wood can be used as a "carbon-
neutral" fuel if more wood is grown
to replace it. An old technique called
coppicing involves cutting wood from
a living tree and allowing new shoots
to sprout from the trunk. When the
firewood is burned it releases its
carbon as carbon dioxide, but this is
soaked up by the regrowing timber.

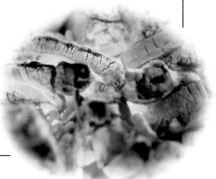

Fossil fern in coal

Fossil Fuels

FOR THOUSANDS OF YEARS, timber was the main fuel used for heating, cooking, and—in the form of charcoal—industrial processes like metalworking. But in the 1700s, people started mining coal, which is a more concentrated, abundant source of energy. Coal fueled the rise of modern industry, as well as the railroads and steamships of the 1800s. In the 1900s oil and natural gas were developed into fuels for road vehicles and aircraft, and both coal and gas are used to generate the electricity that powers our modern lives. All these are carbon-rich "fossil fuels," created from long-dead organisms by processes that take millions of years. They are being burned far more quickly than they are formed, releasing carbon back into the atmosphere and adding to the greenhouse effect.

STORED SUNLIGHT
Fossil fuels are the remains of living things that were buried underground before they had time to decay. Coal is made of plants, so it contains the remains of the carbohydrates they created using the energy of sunlight. So coal is stored solar energy, compacted over millions of years.

COAL MINING
Where coal is found close to the surface it can be extracted from open-pit mines, which create huge holes in the landscape like this one in Wyoming. Deeper coal seams are exploited by sinking deep shafts leading to tunnels, where miners use special machinery to cut the coal out.

OIL AND GAS
Oil is a hydrocarbon, an organic compound containing only the elements hydrogen and carbon. It is found in rocks that were formed on shallow sea floors and is made up of the remains of microscopic marine plankton like these diatoms, which were buried and compressed in the same way as coal-forming plants. The same process that produces oil also creates natural gas, which is mostly methane.

In the 1800s, factories relied on coal for power

INDUSTRIAL REVOLUTION
Coal transformed industry by providing an abundant, portable source of energy. People did not like the smoke and soot pollution it caused, but some enjoyed the wealth it created. Manufacturing industries flourished, leading to the growth of towns and cities, and liberating people from relying on the land to supply their needs. Coal created modern society.

DRILLING FOR OIL

The world's first oil well was sunk at Baku on the shores of the Caspian Sea in 1847. But the oil industry did not take off until the early 1900s, when a refined form of oil began to be used as a fuel for cars. Today oil and gas are tapped from reserves all over the world, on land and beneath shallow seas, where it is pumped up from below the sea bed by oil platforms like this one in the North Sea.

Helicopter landing pad

Drilling rig bores oil well in sea bed

Waste gas is burned off

Long legs support the platform

Spiral roads provide access for giant trucks

Massive excavators dig out the coal

RELEASING THE ENERGY

Burning coal, or any fossil fuel, releases its energy as heat. But it also combines its carbon with oxygen to form carbon dioxide. This accelerates part of the carbon cycle by oxidizing masses of ancient carbon that would naturally be recycled over millions of years. The carbon dioxide pours into the atmosphere much faster than it can be soaked up by the processes that formed the fuel in the first place, so the concentration of carbon dioxide in the air increases.

DIRTY COAL

Different fossil fuels release different quantities of carbon dioxide. Coal is the worst, followed by oil, then gas. Coal also contains other pollutants such as soot and sulfur dioxide, which can combine with water vapor to form smog and acid rain. In 1952 the dense smog seen here killed up to 12,000 people in London, England, and this led to coal fires being banned in the city.

Our carbon culture

MODERN SOCIETY RUNS on fossil fuels. We use them to power our cars, trucks, trains, ships, and aircraft. They run our industries, heat our houses, hospitals, and schools, and generate most of our electricity. Oil is also transformed into the plastics that form part of virtually everything we buy, from food packaging to computers. It is hard to imagine how we could function without them. But our dependence on fossil fuels is the main reason why so much carbon dioxide is being pumped into the atmosphere, increasing the greenhouse effect and causing global warming.

HEAT
In countries with cold winters, people burn fuel to keep warm. Some use open coal fires, but most houses now have central heating fueled by coal, oil, gas, or electricity. Gas is also widely used for cooking. Some electricity is generated without using fossil fuels, but all the other systems use them and release carbon dioxide, contributing to climate change.

Local substation

Transformer reduces voltage

Power distributed to schools, stores, and houses

Steam turbine drives generator that produces electricity

Condenser turns steam back into water

Boiler produces high-pressure steam

Power lines carry electricity over long distances

Coal fuels the boiler

Transformer increases voltage

Cooling tower cools the water in the condenser

POWER PLANT
A huge proportion of the electricity generated in industrialized countries is produced using fossil fuels. In the US, for example, more than three quarters of the total is generated using coal, gas, and oil. In a power plant the fuel is used to heat a boiler that turns water to steam. The steam is fed to a turbine at high pressure, and the spinning turbine turns the electricity generator. The steam from the turbine is cooled to turn it back into water for the boiler.

POWER HUNGRY
A coal-fired power plant uses a huge amount of fuel. The Kingston plant in Tennessee, for example, generates enough electricity to supply 700,000 homes. To meet this demand, it burns over 13,800 tons of coal every day—enough to fill 140 of these big rail trucks. Over the year, this adds up to more than 51,000 trucks full of coal, which would form a train over 310 miles (500 km) long.

Boeing 767

VITAL SUPPLIES

We consume vast amounts of electricity to power transportation, lighting, heating, and air-conditioning systems, as well as domestic equipment. Computers are useless without electricity, and virtually everything we now do or buy involves computers of some kind. The world's banks, businesses, and even governments rely on electronic communications, while transportation control rooms like this one could not operate without them. Electricity also powers the systems that keep us supplied with vital things like food and clean water.

ON THE ROAD

Since the car was invented at the end of the 1800s, we have come to rely on it. Nearly all cars run on hydrocarbon fuels made from oil. Their engines are much more efficient than they used to be, but their average fuel consumption has not improved because most of them are so heavy and powerful. In 1910, 2.2 gallons (10 liters) of gasoline would take the Model "T" Ford shown above almost 56 miles (90 km). The same amount of fuel would carry the average modern American car just 46 miles (74 km).

RAIL TRANSPORTATION

Although coal-fired steam engines are obsolete, many railroads still use diesel or diesel-electric locomotives like this one in the United States, which run on fossil fuel. Most electrified lines use power generated by burning fossil fuels, including coal, so ultimately many electric trains are still fueled by coal. However, railroads use fuel more efficiently than road transportation, especially when carrying heavy goods. Transporting 2,200 lb (1,000 kg) of freight 60 miles (100 km) by road produces about 40 lb (18 kg) of carbon dioxide, while taking them by train emits just 3.3 lb (1.5 kg).

Jet engine emits carbon dioxide and other pollutants

AIR TRAVEL

Jet aircraft are major producers of carbon dioxide and other harmful emissions such as nitrous oxides. These other emissions have an especially serious impact because they are released at such high altitude. Short-haul flights are particularly inefficient because more of the trip is spent gaining height with the engines at full power. A flight of 186 miles (300 km) emits up to 12 times as much carbon dioxide, per passenger, as traveling by train.

FOOD MILES

A lot of our food comes from abroad, because some of it cannot be produced closer to home. Bananas, for example, grow only in tropical climates, so they have to be imported by cooler countries. But we also import foods that can be produced by local farmers, mostly when the local produce is out of season. Transporting all this food can use a lot of fuel, especially if it is air-freighted.

Adding to the problem

DEFORESTATION AND THE USE of fossil fuels are not the only human activities causing climate change. Other aspects of modern life are adding to the problem. Some produce more carbon dioxide, as well as other greenhouse gases such as methane, nitrous oxide, and chlorofluorocarbons (CFCs). These other greenhouse gases are released in much smaller quantities than carbon dioxide, but they have a serious impact because they are much more powerful. A molecule of methane, for example, has the same effect as 25 molecules of carbon dioxide. Soot and other cloudy forms of air pollution also affect the climate by reflecting or absorbing sunlight, causing cooling as well as warming.

CATTLE RANCHING
Our appetite for beef has caused a big increase in cattle ranching, especially in the tropics. But cows produce a lot of methane gas as they digest their food, releasing up to 98,420,000 tons worldwide each year.

Beef burger

RICE GROWING
About 10–15 percent of total global methane emissions come from rice fields. Microbes in the wet soil of flooded paddy fields absorb carbon released by rice plants and turn it into methane, which then seeps into the atmosphere.

Food waste releases methane

CEMENT AND CARBON
Cement production plants like this one make cement from limestone, in a process that turns the rock into calcium oxide and carbon dioxide. It involves pulverizing the limestone and heating it to about 2,640°F (1,450°C), which uses a lot of fuel. Cement is very heavy, so transporting it also uses a lot of fuel. Altogether, producing and shipping each bag of cement releases roughly the same weight of carbon dioxide into the atmosphere.

Plastic and metal do not rot down

LANDFILL
Developed countries generate immense quantities of garbage. A lot of it gets burned, releasing carbon dioxide and other, more noxious gases. But a lot more is buried in "landfill sites" where the normal decay process is inhibited by lack of air. Instead, the food waste and other organic remains are broken down by bacteria that do not need oxygen. These return carbon to the air in the form of methane, which is an extremely potent greenhouse gas—so even burying garbage is helping to cause global warming.

NITROUS OXIDE
This is a relatively scarce, but extremely potent gas, about 300 times as powerful as carbon dioxide. While it is produced naturally by bacteria in the soil, exposed soil may release twice the usual amount. It is also released from the artificial fertilizer that farmers spread on their fields.

Fridges are degassed before being scrapped

Trucks collect garbage from towns and cities

CHLOROFLUOROCARBONS (CFCs)
A variety of artificial gases are now known to be potent greenhouse gases. They include the CFCs that were once used as refrigerants in domestic fridges. When old fridges are discarded, they must have the gas carefully removed to stop it from escaping into the atmosphere.

AEROSOLS
Some forms of air pollution create clouds of small particles known as aerosols. These can reflect or absorb sunlight and reduce its power. This has reduced the impact of the human-enhanced greenhouse effect over recent decades. But aerosols do not stay airborne for long, so reducing air pollution could actually accelerate warming.

Garbage is dumped, compressed, and covered over

SURFACE REFLECTANCE
Airborne soot has been carried to the Arctic, where it settles on snow and ice, making it darker so it does not reflect so much sunlight. It absorbs the energy instead, and this makes it warm up. This is helping to raise temperatures in the Arctic, melting snow and floating sea ice.

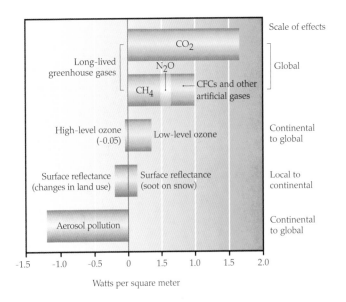

WARMING AND COOLING
This chart shows the main causes of climate change and how much they contribute to the change. Warming factors include carbon dioxide (CO_2), methane (CH_4), nitrous oxide (N_2O), artificial gases such as CFCs, and low-level ozone. Soot pollution on snow is also a warming factor. Change of land use and aerosol pollution have a cooling effect, shown in blue.

Heatwaves and droughts

By STUDYING WEATHER AND CLIMATE DATA gathered from all over the world, and transmitted from orbiting satellites, scientists can compare it with past records to work out how much the world has warmed up. But for many people, the evidence of climate change is much more obvious. They are suffering heatwaves that can raise temperatures to lethal levels, and living with droughts that make drinking water scarce, kill their crops and farm animals, and turn fertile land to desert. Some of the droughts may be caused by natural cycles, and deserts can be partly created by poor farming methods such as overgrazing by livestock. But there is little doubt that periods of seriously hot or dry weather are getting more frequent.

GOES-12

WEATHER SATELLITE
Launched in July 2001, the GOES-12 environmental satellite is one of many orbiting spacecraft equipped with remote sensors for monitoring weather conditions in the lower atmosphere, 22,370 miles (36,000 km) below the satellite.

HEATWAVES
Higher extreme temperatures are becoming more common. They are not always the highest daytime temperatures known since records began, but long periods of sustained high temperatures known as heatwaves. During the European heatwave of August 2003, Paris suffered nine days in a row with temperatures above 95°F (35°C). Aug 10 of that year was the hottest day ever recorded in London, peaking at 100.6°F (38.1°C), and 117.1°F (47.3°C) was recorded at Amareleja in Portugal. Here a fountain in Prague helps a woman cool down during a heatwave that hit the Czech Republic in July 2007.

THE HUMAN TOLL
Heat can be a killer, especially when it continues through the day and night. In the US, people cope with heat by using air conditioning—which itself contributes to climate change. In regions where people are not equipped to deal with the heat, they are more vulnerable. The elderly are the first to suffer, like this victim of a heatwave in Chicago in 2006, because their bodies cannot lose heat easily. In Rome, Italy, half the city's 700 casualties of the 2003 European heatwave were over 85 years old—and the heat is believed to have killed as many as 50,000 people throughout Europe.

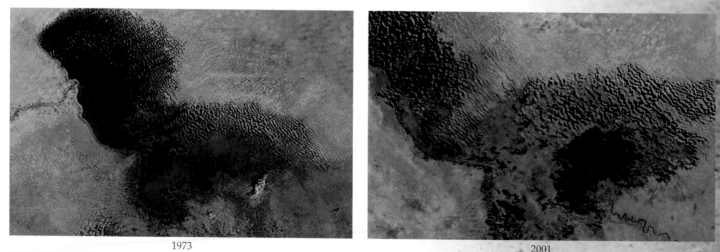

1973

2001

SHRINKING LAKES
Heat makes water evaporate from the ground surface, drying the soil. If this moisture is not replaced by rainfall, the level of groundwater sinks, draining the water from lakes. People often make the problem worse by diverting water into irrigation schemes designed to revive wilting crops. Over the last 40 years, a combination of these factors has caused the near-disappearance of Lake Chad on the southern fringes of the Sahara. The lake is seen here in two satellite views taken 26 years apart. Once the sixth-largest lake in the world, it is now one twentieth of its original size.

DESERTIFICATION

If there is not enough rain to make up for the evaporation of water from the ground, the soil can gradually turn to dust. This process can be accelerated or even caused by poor farming methods, as happened in the Great Plains states in the 1930s, or more recently in the Sahel region on the southern fringes of the Sahara in Africa. But if rainfall dwindles to below the critical level, even well-managed land will turn to desert. This may be happening in eastern and southeastern Australia, where the rainfall of 2006 was among the lowest on record. Low rainfall is also causing the expansion of the central Asian Gobi Desert, driving dust storms across huge areas of China and Mongolia. This Mongolian woman is carrying water to her home during one of the dust storms.

Scarf protects the woman from airborne dust during the storm

DRIED-UP RIVERS

Reduced rainfall is making some rivers dry up. In 2005 they included the greatest river of all, the Amazon, which suffered its worst drought in 40 years. Many of its tributaries shrank to a fraction of their normal width, exposing broad areas of dried, cracked mud littered with dead fish. The Rio Negro, the main northern tributary of the Amazon, was reduced to its lowest level since records began in 1902.

DROUGHT AND FAMINE

Many people who live on the dry fringes of deserts rely on seasonal rains to make their crops grow and provide water for their farm animals. If these rains fail owing to changed weather patterns, the crops and animals may die, as seen here in southern Ethiopia in 2006. This leaves the people with nothing to eat, and facing the threat of famine.

WILDFIRES

The firefighters on top of this house are desperately trying to save it from a forest fire that ignited during very hot and dry weather. In dry regions such as Australia, many plants are able to cope with regular fires, but during long droughts, the risk of fire can spread to areas where the vegetation is not adapted to survive it. In parts of Amazonia, a combination of drought and deforestation is making the ground so dry that wildfires are raging through forests that have never suffered them before.

Melting ice

IN COLD CLIMATES snow builds up and gradually becomes compacted into virtually solid ice, forming mountain glaciers and polar ice sheets. Polar oceans also freeze at the surface in winter, creating floating pack ice. But a lot of this ice is melting. Arctic pack ice is shrinking, vast Antarctic ice shelves are collapsing, and mountain glaciers are retreating. On the polar fringes, higher temperatures are also melting ice that lies beneath the ground, transforming tundra landscapes.

Ice acts like a mirror, reflecting solar energy

Dark water absorbs energy and gets warmer

ACCELERATING THE MELT
Glittering white sea ice reflects most of the Sun's energy. But if it melts, it gives way to dark ocean water, which absorbs most of the energy and warms up, melting more ice. This positive feedback effect is probably increasing the rate of Arctic sea ice melting.

SHRINKING SEA ICE
In winter most of the Arctic Ocean is covered with a sheet of floating ice up to 10 ft (3 m) thick, and roughly the size of the United States. Half of this area melts in summer, leaving the central Arctic Ocean still icy. Since 1979 the size of this summer ice sheet has dwindled by about 600,000 sq miles (1.5 million sq km)—an area about twice the size of Texas. During the 1990s its average thickness also decreased by 3 ft 4 in (1 m).

Iceberg has broken off floating edge of ice sheet

GREENLAND
Most of Greenland is covered by a huge ice sheet, more than 1.9 miles (3 km) thick at its center. Every summer the edges of the ice get thinner, and the area affected by this is increasing. The glaciers that flow from the ice sheet to the sea are also moving faster, increasing the rate at which icebergs break away and melt. Both of these processes are causing the sea level to rise.

MELTING PERMAFROST
About a quarter of the land in the Northern Hemisphere is so cold that it is permanently frozen beneath the surface. This permafrost is covered by a surface layer that is frozen in winter but thaws in summer, creating vast areas of swampland. In many areas of the lower Arctic, the active surface layer is getting deeper each year, melting ancient ice and undermining buildings like this house in Irkutsk, Siberia, which is slowly sinking into the ground.

RETREATING GLACIERS

Glaciers form as snow builds up over the years, packing down to form rivers of ice that creep slowly downhill, scouring deep U-shaped valleys. In the polar regions, many glaciers flow all the way to the sea, where ice breaks off to form icebergs. But most glaciers that form in high, cold mountain valleys turn to streams and lakes of meltwater long before they reach the coast. All over the world, rising temperatures are making these mountain glaciers melt away at their lower, warmer ends, which retreat uphill to where temperatures are lower. The retreat can be dramatic, as shown by these two images of the Upsala glacier in Patagonia, South America—the upper photograph was taken in 1928, and the lower one in 2004.

ANTARCTICA

Antarctica is covered by a colossal ice sheet up to 2.8 miles (4.5 km) thick, and covering an area of 5.4 million sq miles (14 million sq km). It consists of the huge east Antarctic ice sheet, east of the Transantarctic Mountains, which seems to be gaining ice, and the smaller west Antarctic ice sheet which is losing ice. The ice is melting fastest on the Antarctic Peninsula, where temperatures are rising more rapidly than anywhere else on Earth, by up to 5.4°F (3°C) since 1951.

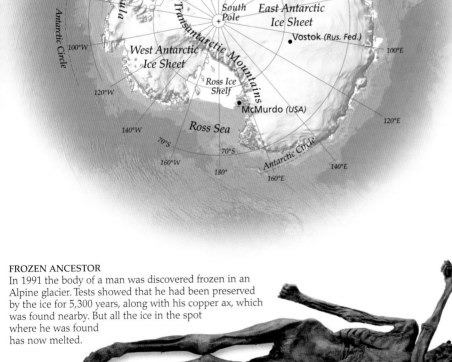

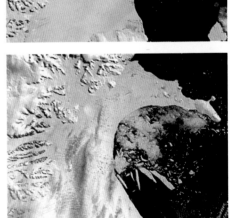

COLLAPSING ICE SHELVES

In early 2002, 1,250 sq miles (3,250 sq km) of the 650-ft (200-m) thick Larsen-B ice shelf near the tip of the Antarctic Peninsula disintegrated within 35 days, and the fragments drifted away as icebergs. These satellite images show blue pools of meltwater forming on the surface on January 31 (top), and the ice shelf collapsing 23 days later.

FROZEN ANCESTOR

In 1991 the body of a man was discovered frozen in an Alpine glacier. Tests showed that he had been preserved by the ice for 5,300 years, along with his copper ax, which was found nearby. But all the ice in the spot where he was found has now melted.

Warming oceans

RISING SEA LEVELS
As ocean water warms up, it expands like the liquid in a thermometer, so sea levels rise by a small amount. But gauges like this show a much greater actual rise, indicating that melting ice is adding to the problem.

THE EFFECTS OF RISING GLOBAL TEMPERATURES are often dramatic on land, causing heatwaves, wildfires, and vanishing glaciers, but their impact on the oceans is less obvious. So far the oceans have not warmed as much as the continents. This is partly because they warm up more slowly. In fact the heat that they have absorbed will make deep oceans keep warming even if all greenhouse gas emissions stopped tomorrow. This will make the ocean water expand, raising sea levels. Meltwater from continental ice sheets is also pouring into the oceans, making sea levels rise much more. Warmer water at the ocean surface reduces plankton growth and carbon dioxide absorption. It also causes more intense storms that sweep over nearby continents, sometimes with catastrophic effects.

MELTWATER
The extra water that is making sea levels rise is coming from melting glaciers and continental ice sheets. If floating sea ice melts, this makes no difference to sea level because the floating ice is already in the sea, and simply changes from solid to liquid. But when ice on land melts, the water that it contains is transferred to the ocean. If this glacier melts away completely, all its water will flow into the sea.

Icebergs are floating lumps of glacier ice

ICEBERGS
In the polar regions, and in a few other places, glaciers flow all the way to the sea. The ends of these glaciers are floating, so when lumps of ice break off, they drift away as floating icebergs. Some of these icebergs are huge, and since they float with up to 90 percent of their bulk underwater, they are all much bigger than they look. They can raise sea levels in the same way as meltwater, whether they melt or stay solid. They can also be a serious hazard to shipping.

FLOODED OUT
Rising sea levels have already started destroying the coral island nation of Tuvalu in the Pacific, where most of the land lies just 6–10 ft (2–3 m) above sea level. Higher tides are making waves surge further inland, swamping houses and contaminating farmland and water supplies with salt water. Since sea levels are expected to keep rising for 1,000 years after all greenhouse gas emissions stop—and for longer if they don't stop —the 11,000 citizens of Tuvalu will have to evacuate their islands, almost certainly forever. Other low-lying nations such as the Maldives are just as vulnerable.

Deep-water circulation

Cooled, salty, dense water sinks in the north Atlantic

Warm, salty surface water flows north

Atlantic deepwater current flows south

Deep water is drawn to the surface in north Pacific Ocean

Deep water is drawn to the surface in Indian Ocean

Warm surface current flows west across tropical Pacific Ocean

CURRENT SLOWDOWN

Dense, salty water at the surface of the northern Atlantic sinks and pushes currents through the deeper parts of the world's oceans. But melting icebergs, glaciers, and permafrost add fresh water to the oceans, making them less salty, and this affects the mechanism that drives the deepwater currents. The north Atlantic deepwater flow could slow by up to half over the coming century, disrupting the global circulation of water.

Hurricane structure

High-level winds swirl outward

Cold, dense, deepwater current flows into Pacific Ocean

Air descends in the eye, an area of calm at the center

Strongest winds swirl around the eye of the storm

Sea surface rises at center of hurricane

Warm, moist air rises, forming thick clouds

HURRICANES AND CYCLONES

Storms that build up over oceans can cause havoc if they reach land. The storms develop because the Sun's heat causes warm, moist air to rise, creating an area of low pressure at the water's surface, and thick clouds above it. The low pressure draws in more air, which forms a circular wind system called a cyclone. Over tropical oceans cyclones can develop into destructive hurricanes.

CO2 SATURATION POINT

About one quarter of the carbon dioxide that we add to the air is absorbed by the oceans. It dissolves in the water and a lot is taken up by marine plankton. However, most warm oceans do not contain much plankton, and the oceans are getting warmer. The stormy Southern Ocean around Antarctica—seen here swamping the deck of a racing yacht—also appears to be so loaded with carbon dioxide that it cannot absorb any more. This could be a serious problem, because it accounts for 15 percent of the carbon dioxide soaked up by oceans each year.

SWAMPED CITIES

More intense storms caused by warmer oceans seem to be increasing rainfall in the temperate north by 5–10 percent, causing floods like those that hit England in 2007. Unusually heavy rain has also struck the tropics. The deluge shown here occurred in July 2005, when a massive 37 in (944 mm) of rain fell on Mumbai, India, in 24 hours—50 percent more than the previous record.

DATA FROM THE DEEP
Ocean currents have a powerful influence on climate because they redistribute heat around the globe. These sampling bottles gather water samples from different depths, so scientists can record their temperature and chemistry. This enables them to work out if and how current flow patterns are changing.

Oceanic research

A LOT OF CLIMATE RESEARCH takes place at sea, because the dynamics of the ocean are a major part of the overall climate system. Every day scientists work hard to gather data that enhances our understanding of the way the system works, and how the oceans and atmosphere interact to influence climate change. Much of this data is obtained by sophisticated technology, including remote sensors on automated buoys, miniature submersibles, and even satellites.

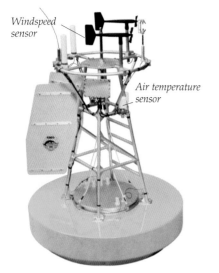

Windspeed sensor

Air temperature sensor

RESEARCH SHIP
The British research ship RRS *James Cook* is one of several dedicated research vessels used by scientists to study oceans and climate at first hand throughout the world. With a crew of 22, it has facilities for 32 scientists specializing in every aspect of ocean research, from oceanic weather patterns to the geology of the ocean floor. The ship can stay at sea for 50 days, so it can work in the deep oceans as well as coastal waters, from the tropics to the fringes of the polar ice. Satellite links allow the scientists to exchange data with research institutions worldwide.

Satellite communications

Scientific crane

Equipment gantry

SURFACE MEASUREMENTS
Understanding how the atmosphere and ocean interact is vital to the study of climates. This research buoy is one of many that collect essential data such as air and sea temperature, atmospheric pressure, and wind speed, and transmit the data to a research base ship.

REEF ANALYSIS
This diver is extracting a core sample from a Pacific coral island, so that the growth of the coral reef can be analysed. Patterns of coral growth over the centuries provide a valuable insight into the oceanic climates of the past, and they also mark fluctuations in sea level.

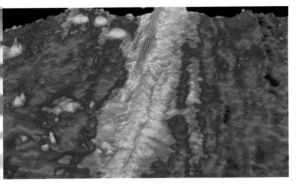

ACOUSTIC PROBE

Since the 1960s oceanographers have been using sound signals to generate detailed three-dimensional maps of the ocean floor, revealing features like this long submarine ridge in the Pacific. This information is vital to research into ocean currents, since computers can now model the interaction of flowing water with the ocean floor. Sound waves are also affected by water temperature, so they can be used to detect both the flow of warm and cold water through the oceans, and fluctuations that may be linked to global warming.

OCEAN ECOLOGY

Clouds of oceanic plankton like this in the Baltic absorb a lot of the carbon dioxide that we pump into the atmosphere, and turn it into food for other ocean life. With satellite sensing, scientists can monitor the global distribution and abundance of plankton, and see how it is responding to climate change.

Microscopic single-celled organisms form a vast green cloud

Satellite image of the. Baltic Sea

Navigation station

Meteorology platform

Glider is battery-powered

BENEATH THE WAVES

Automated "underwater gliders" such as this cruise silently below the water's surface, gathering data over vast distances. Able to operate independently for a month, they are equipped with sensors for detecting and measuring waves, currents, and many of the other variables that scientists use to assess the ocean's role in climate change. At intervals the gliders surface to relay the data through satellite links to oceanographic laboratories on land.

Ship is named after the famous British explorer and navigator Captain James Cook (1728–1779)

Living with the heat

IN THE LONG TERM, wildlife evolves to cope with both cooler and warmer climates. However, evolution is a harsh process. Many plants and animals cannot cope with the change and eventually become extinct. Meanwhile other organisms flourish because they adapt and develop features that enable them to survive. The result is a new mix of species to suit an altered world. This process enabled the mammals to take over when the dinosaurs became extinct 65 million years ago. Recent wildlife losses may be signaling that we are at the beginning of a similar process now.

OVERHEATED REEFS
As tropical oceans get warmer, coral reefs start to suffer. The corals that build reefs live in partnership with microscopic organisms that grow in their tissues and make food by photosynthesis. But if the water gets too warm, the corals expel the colorful microbes and turn white, like the coral in this picture. Corals can survive brief periods of this coral bleaching, but if the water stays too warm, they start running out of food and dying. Rising ocean temperatures will probably cause more bleaching events, threatening vulnerable corals with extinction.

Long antennae could snap more easily

Shell is reinforced with alkaline calcium

Powerful claw relies on strong shell

ACIDIFIED OCEANS
When rain dissolves atmospheric carbon dioxide, it forms a weak carbonic acid. The same process is affecting the oceans as they absorb extra carbon dioxide from the air. It is not making the oceans acid, but it is making them less alkaline. The change could start to make life difficult for many marine animals such as corals, clams, and this lobster, which absorb alkaline minerals from the water to build their tough shells.

STARVING SEABIRDS
The oceanic food chain relies on the drifting microlife of the plankton which feeds the fish that are caught by hunters such as seabirds. Warmer oceans are changing the distribution of plankton, so fish move away from seabird nesting sites. In the north Atlantic, colonies of seabirds like these guillemots are failing because they cannot feed their young.

DISAPPEARING WETLANDS
As droughts become more common and human populations grow and use more water, wetlands such as marshes and lakes are starting to dry up. These wetlands are vital to many animals, not only as places to live, but also as sources of drinking water, so their disappearance can be catastrophic for wildlife. Here scientists studying the effects of changing water levels in a Florida swamp wade up to their waists to gather samples.

UPHILL MIGRANTS
Many plants and animals are adapted for survival on high mountains where it is too cold for trees to grow. As temperatures rise, the trees creep slowly uphill, forcing the mountain species uphill too. Eventually they may run out of space and become locally extinct. In the Himalayas, as illustrated here, all the animals will steadily extend their ranges uphill.

Bearded vulture

Snow leopard

Tundra

Takin

Alpine grassland

Low-growing shrubs

Asiatic ass

Cool coniferous forest

Red panda

Hanuman langur

Temperate deciduous forest

Subtropical deciduous forest

EARLY LOSSES
Climate change may have already made some animals extinct. The golden toad was discovered in the Monteverde cloud forests of Costa Rica as recently as 1966. In 1987 it was common, but two years later it had virtually disappeared, and by 1991 it was deemed extinct. The toads' young were attacked by a fungal disease that started to flourish as the nights became warmer, so when the adult toads died, there were no young ones to take their place.

MIGRATIONS AND EXPANSIONS
Some animals seem to be adapting to climate change. Insects have short lifespans and rapid breeding rates, enabling them to evolve quickly, and many are able to move into new habitats easily. They include disease-carrying mosquitoes, which are spreading diseases such as malaria and West Nile virus to areas that were once too cold for the insects.

Malarial mosquitoes kill over a million people a year

OUT OF STEP
Rising temperatures can disrupt the balance of nature. In Europe, woodland caterpillars are hatching two weeks earlier in spring, and birds returning from Africa to breed arrive after most of the caterpillars have gone. They struggle to find food, and their young may starve.

Plight of the polar bear

CLIMATE CHANGE IS A SERIOUS PROBLEM for the animals that hunt or breed on the sea ice of the Arctic. The ice is shrinking each year, and the summer ice may disappear completely by 2070, or even earlier. The most vulnerable of these animals is the species right at the top of the food chain —the polar bear. It feeds mainly on seals, which eat fish that feed on smaller fish and crustaceans. If the warming of the Arctic Ocean disrupts this food chain, all the animals will suffer, but polar bears will suffer most because it takes a huge number of crustaceans, fish, and seals to support just one bear. Polar bears are also specialized for hunting on the sea ice, so if the ice vanishes, the bears may vanish too.

SEA BEAR
The polar bear evolved about 250,000 years ago from the grizzly bear to become a specialized Arctic hunter. It lives on the pack ice on the surface of the Arctic Ocean, but favors the thinner, yet stable ice that forms in winter around the fringes of the thick, permanent ice near the North Pole. It wanders over vast areas of the frozen ocean, but it can also swim for several hours to cross stretches of open water. Either way it spends most of its life at sea.

OCEANIC HUNTER
The polar bear's main prey are ringed seals and bearded seals. It catches the adult seals when they come up through holes in the sea ice to breathe. It is an expert at detecting these breathing holes by scent, locating them from up to 0.6 mile (one kilometer) away. In early summer the bear sniffs out the snow-covered ice caves of ringed seal pups, and breaks through the ice to catch them.

Ringed seal

WINTER NURSERY
When the pack ice melts, polar bears find hunting difficult and may not eat for four months or more until the sea freezes in the fall. Pregnant females retreat to snow dens where they have their cubs in midwinter, feeding them on their rich milk until they emerge onto the ice in spring.

SHRINKING ICE
Rising temperatures mean that large areas of ocean that once stayed frozen throughout the year now become open water with a few scattered ice floes. Polar bears often have to swim long distances between areas of stable ice. The ice also melts earlier in summer. This forces the bears ashore, often before they have eaten enough to build up the thick fat reserves that allow them to survive without eating until the sea freezes again.

DESPERATE REMEDIES

Polar bears are badly equipped for hunting on land, and when the pack ice melts in summer, hungry bears often enter northern towns in search of food. They are big, dangerous animals, so this can lead to trouble. If bears become too much of a nuisance around towns, they may be tranquilized and airlifted to places further north where there is still enough pack ice for them to hunt at sea.

Polar Bear Compound

POLLUTION AND POISONING

Hungry polar bears often scavenge near human settlements. They frequently raid garbage dumps, where they may eat things that they should not. They naturally eat a lot of fat to build up their own energy-rich fat reserves, and starving bears have been seen eating dumped industrial grease and even motor oil. Many bears are also becoming slowly poisoned through eating prey contaminated by pollution, partly because a lot of the pollution was locked up in Arctic ice that is now melting.

A BLEAK FUTURE

If the Arctic sea ice disappears completely in summer, the future for polar bears looks bleak. The seals that they prey upon will become scarce as they lose their icy breeding habitat. Female bears may not be able to find enough food to see them through the winter when they nurse their young. Unable to hunt effectively on land, many bears will just starve. So it is likely that the polar bear will become extinct in the wild, with just a few surviving in zoos.

Predicting the future has never been easy. It is clear that adding more greenhouse gases to the atmosphere will make the planet warmer, but how much warmer will it get, and what effects will this have on the world? There are a lot of factors to consider, and scientists try to take account of them all by building them into mathematical "models" of the climate, and using computers to see what happens when the figures for greenhouse gas emissions are increased. The resulting projections agree that if we do nothing to stop climate change, temperatures could rise by 5.4°F (3°C) or more by 2100—with potentially serious results.

COMPUTER POWER

Computers have been used for many decades to forecast the changes in the atmosphere that control day-to-day weather. Doing the same for long-term climate change is more difficult, because there are extra factors to consider such as changes in vegetation and ice cover. But supercomputers like these can process vast amounts of data, and every year the computers become more powerful and, more importantly, our understanding of climate improves.

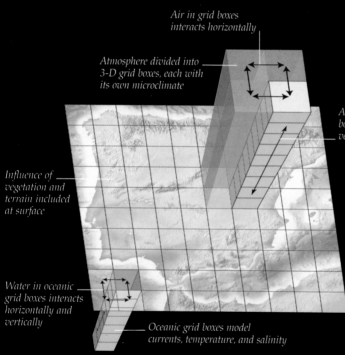

Air in grid boxes interacts horizontally

Atmosphere divided into 3-D grid boxes, each with its own microclimate

Air in grid boxes interacts vertically

Influence of vegetation and terrain included at surface

Water in oceanic grid boxes interacts horizontally and vertically

Oceanic grid boxes model currents, temperature, and salinity

CLIMATE MODELING

A climate model is a computerized representation of the atmosphere based on a three-dimensional global grid. This is linked to submodels that represent other global systems such as the oceans, as shown here, or vegetation growth. The computer program allows some factors to be changed, such as the amount of carbon dioxide in the atmosphere or the degree of pollution from airborne particles or aerosols. The model then applies these changes to its virtual world, to see what effect they have on the climate.

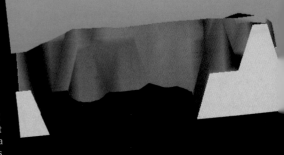

South America

South American continental shelf

RUNNING THE MODEL

When it is run on the computer, a climate model evolves in a series of short time steps, often of less than an hour each, and each step may take a few seconds to process. So achieving a projection to the end of the century takes several weeks, even when using one of the most powerful supercomputers. The results can then be used to generate graphs and images that show how temperatures and rainfall might change in different circumstances. This three-dimensional image has been generated from a model of changing global sea temperatures.

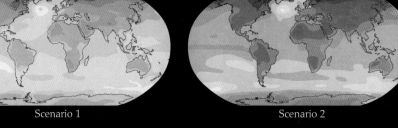

Scenario 1   Scenario 2

DIFFERENT SCENARIOS

Each climate model is based on a different "scenario." These cover the various ways in which the world might develop. The basic scenario assumes steady economic growth and a corresponding increase in greenhouse gas emissions. Others might include a major switch away from them. These globes show predicted temperature rises by 2090-2099 based on two scenarios: a less industrialized world than today's world (1) and a world with rapid economic growth (2).

TEMPERATURE CHANGE (°C)

0.0 0.5 1.0 1.5 2.0 2.5 3.0 3.5 4.0 4.5 5.0 5.5 6.0 6.5

CONFIDENCE AND UNCERTAINTY

Climate projections are a bit like long-range weather forecasts. However, they focus on the long-term averages of the whole system and how these change, rather than the day-to-day local variations that make detailed weather forecasting so difficult. So even if we cannot forecast the weather for next week, we can be confident that continued greenhouse gas emissions will lead to higher temperatures at the end of this century. But since it is hard to take account of all the variables, different modeling labs come up with different projections. This graph shows eight projections made by seven labs, using the same basic scenario that little is done to reduce greenhouse gas emissions.

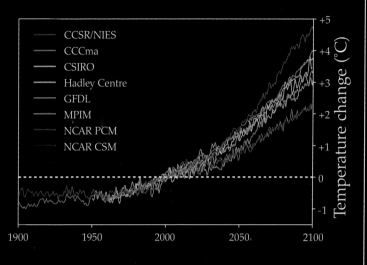

— CCSR/NIES
— CCCma
— CSIRO
— Hadley Centre
— GFDL
— MPIM
— NCAR PCM
— NCAR CSM

North America

Greenland

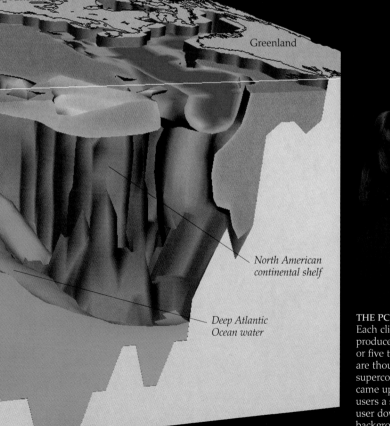

North American continental shelf

Deep Atlantic Ocean water

TEMPERATURE CHANGE (°F)

-0.5 -0.4 -0.3 -0.2 -0.1 0.0 +0.1 +0.2 +0.3 +0.4 +0.5

THE PC SOLUTION

Each climate model takes weeks to run through to the end of the century and produce a climate projection. Models based on four or five scenarios take four or five times as long, and because there are so many different variables, there are thousands of possible scenarios. Faced with this problem, even the biggest supercomputers run out of capacity. In 2003 UK climate analyst Myles Allen came up with a solution—to offer thousands of home or school computer users a simplified version of a climate model that runs on a standard PC. Each user downloads a model based on a slightly different scenario. It runs as a background task whenever the computer is switched on, and can even display its current results as a screensaver. Running each model to the end takes several months, but since thousands of computers are working at once, they generate a lot of results more quickly than a few overloaded supercomputers.

The next century

THE GLOBAL AVERAGE temperature is certain to rise during the 21st century. Even if we were able to stop adding greenhouse gases to the atmosphere, the heat stored in the oceans would continue to be released over several decades. Exactly how this will affect the world is less certain, but there will probably be increasingly frequent and extreme heatwaves, droughts, and floods. More glaciers and polar ice will melt, and fragile natural environments will suffer, causing the extinction of many animals and plants. Some of these impacts are inevitable, but if we try to combat climate change we may be able to limit the damage.

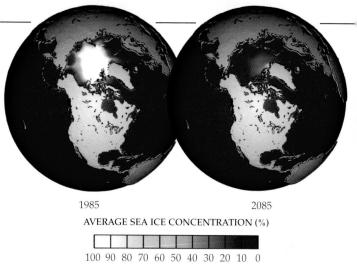

1985   2085

AVERAGE SEA ICE CONCENTRATION (%)

100 90 80 70 60 50 40 30 20 10 0

THE NORTH POLE

These images show the extent of Arctic summer ice in 1985, and its projected extent in 2085. Many scientists believe that by 2070, the thick pack ice that covers the Arctic Ocean at the North Pole could melt away entirely during the Arctic summer, leaving open water. This will be a catastrophe for the ice-breeding seals and polar bears that live in the region. The loss of summer ice and increased flow of fresh meltwater into the sea may also affect the currents that flow around the Arctic Ocean and the north Atlantic. The pack ice will form again in winter, but it will not cover such a broad area as it does now. Meanwhile more and more permafrost will disappear in the far north.

EXPANDING DESERTS

Scientists contributing to the IPCC predict that there will be up to 20 percent less rainfall in most subtropical lands. Many of these regions are already semideserts, so if they get less rain, they will dry out and become deserts. These will spread into neighboring scrubland and grassland, and could start affecting areas that are now farmland, such as the corn belt of the United States and the vineyards of southern Europe. Further north and south, summer heatwaves are likely to become more frequent and extreme.

The Pudong district of Shanghai

VULNERABLE CITIES

Sea levels will keep rising as more glacial meltwater pours into the oceans. By the year 2100, they are likely to be 8–24 in (20–60 cm) higher than they are now, provided that nothing catastrophic happens to the great continental ice sheets of Greenland or Antarctica. This may not seem too threatening, but many of the world's great cities are built on low-lying coasts, and are at risk from flooding. One of the most vulnerable is Shanghai in China—a city of 18 million people built on land that is just 10–16 ft (3–5 m) above sea level. Currently its sea defenses are just adequate to prevent flooding by storms in the East China Sea, but they may not be able to cope as sea levels rise.

STORM WARNING

Hurricanes are likely to become more powerful as ocean surface temperatures rise, and they will probably occur over a wider area of the tropics. Outside the tropics, increased evaporation of water from warmer oceans will also lead to more intense storms over nearby land, causing fast-moving flash floods of the type that devastated Boscastle, England in 2004. These cars were swept out to sea by a wall of water, mud, and rubble that surged down a river valley after an unusually heavy summer thunderstorm.

WILDLIFE EXTINCTIONS

If the average global temperature continues to rise as predicted by scientists, 15 to 37 percent of the world's wild animal and plant species could face extinction by 2050. These will include many specialized organisms, such as polar bears, reef corals, and rare flowers like this clamshell orchid from the Florida Everglades in the US. By contrast, more adaptable living things such as rats and cockroaches may flourish.

SHIFTING VEGETATION ZONES

As the polar regions warm up and the subtropics turn to deserts, wild plants will creep toward the poles. Evergreen trees like these pines will move into treeless Arctic tundra, and in warmer, drier areas, grass will take over from woodland. But large tracts of farmland may prevent this natural migration, and many species of wild plants could simply die out.

What scares the scientists?

IF WE DO NOT MAKE every effort to combat climate change, global temperatures could rise high enough to trigger events like the mass melting of Arctic permafrost, or huge wildfires in Amazonia. These would release more greenhouse gases, accelerating global warming. We know that such catastrophic climate change has happened in the distant past. To stop it from happening again, we must act now, before events move beyond our control.

MELTING THE TUNDRA
Vast areas of the far north are frozen below ground. In summer this permafrost partly thaws, forming huge swamps full of decaying vegetation, as here in Siberia. The decay process releases methane, a greenhouse gas that is 25 times more powerful than carbon dioxide, but a lot of this methane is frozen into the permafrost. As temperatures rise and more permafrost melts each summer, more methane is released, adding to the greenhouse effect.

BURNING RAINFORESTS
Tropical rainforests do not normally suffer wildfires, but as temperatures rise, they are drying out and burning. Even if the trees do not burn, they can die from drought. Trees pump water into the air through their leaves, so fewer trees means less rain. This process could destroy the richest ecosystem on Earth, and as the trees burn or decay, all the carbon in their timber will turn to carbon dioxide, raising temperatures still further.

ACID OCEANS
As oceans get warmer and become more acid through absorbing carbon dioxide, many marine organisms will start to die off. If temperatures rise to 3.6°F (2°C) above pre-industrial levels, up to 97 percent of the world's coral reefs could suffer "coral bleaching" and die. Acidified water may make it impossible for organisms such as crabs, clams, and microscopic plankton to build their shells, and this would destroy the food supply of other animals such as fish. The result could be a mass extinction involving many types of marine life.

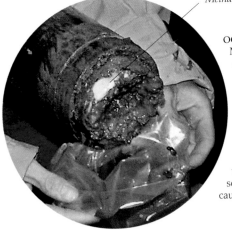

Methane hydrate in a sample of ocean-floor mud

OCEANIC METHANE

Methane seeping from decaying plankton on the ocean floor can combine with very cold water to create a type of ice called methane hydrate. It normally stays frozen, but if the water temperature rises, the hydrate can melt. This releases methane, which then bubbles up through the water into the atmosphere, adding to the greenhouse effect. It will take centuries for the ocean depths to get warm enough for this to happen, but some scientists think that it may have helped cause extreme global warming in the past.

MASSIVE SEA LEVEL RISE

Most scientists think that sea levels will rise by less than four feet (one meter) by 2100. But if the immensely thick ice sheets of Antarctica and Greenland start to collapse in a big way, sea levels could rise by a lot more than this, and ultimately by up to 82 ft (25 m). Even a 23-ft (7-m) rise—the effect of the Greenland ice sheet collapsing—would swamp coastal cities such as London, New York, Tokyo, Shanghai, and Calcutta.

COLLAPSING ICE SHEETS

The fringes of the Greenland and west Antarctic ice sheets are already melting faster than ever recorded before, with huge slabs of ice breaking off and floating away as icebergs. This loss of ice around the fringes will make it easier for blocks of continental ice to slip toward the ocean, lubricated by meltwater seeping down through fissures in the ice. This could allow the ice sheets to collapse, making sea levels rise dramatically.

THE BOTTOM LINE

If we allow global warming to run out of control, then it could eventually wipe out most of life on Earth. This happened about 250 million years ago, when some 96 percent of all species at that time became extinct. Scientists believe that massive volcanic activity caused colossal carbon dioxide release and global warming, reinforced by methane release from oceans. During this event the average temperature appears to have risen by 10.8–14.4°F (6–8°C). Global temperatures could easily increase by 7.2°F (4°C) by 2100—and possibly more.

Climate change and society

LIVING ON THE EDGE
The Inuit hunter in this 19th-century lithograph is waiting for a seal to pop up through a breathing hole. Some Inuits still use the same hunting method today. Like Inuit hunters, people who live in harsh climates have developed ways of life that suit their environments. Climate change could make their skills useless, and their cultures could fall apart.

CLIMATE CHANGE WILL HAVE A BIG IMPACT on human society, even if we manage to slow it down. The people who are likely to suffer most are those who have done least to create the problem—those that live in the developing world. Many already have to cope with extreme climates, where farming and even getting enough drinking water can be difficult. Climate change and its effects will only make life harder, so there are likely to be more famines, mass migrations, and conflicts over land and resources. Low-lying nations may be flooded by rising sea levels, forcing their citizens to leave. Industrialized societies will suffer too, both directly and because of serious problems in other parts of the world.

PEOPLE ON THE MOVE
If land becomes uninhabitable because it has been flooded or has turned to desert, the people who live there will have to leave. The result could be the biggest mass migration in history. It is unlikely that neighboring countries will allow huge numbers of people to simply move in, settle, and produce their own food. The refugees will end up in camps like this one in Ethiopia, relying on foreign aid and living in miserable conditions, with poor sanitation, little to eat, and nothing to do. Whole societies could collapse, and conflicts caused by disputes over land could easily lead to violence, civil war, and famine.

DISEASE
As the world warms up, tropical diseases seem to be spreading. Malaria, which is carried by tropical mosquitoes, now infects about 500 million people a year —four times more than in 1990. Blood tests will reveal if these children have also been infected.

Makeshift tent on roof provides shelter

RISING WATERS
Many highly populated parts of the world lie close to sea level. They include the Ganges Delta region of India and Bangladesh. If climate change causes a sea level rise of just 39 in (1 m), this could flood 17 percent of Bangladesh, forcing millions of people to move out. If a hurricane caused catastrophic flooding on top of this—as it did in 1970—millions could die. Here survivors of a flood in 2004 wait to be rescued from a roof in Dhaka, the capital of Bangladesh.

WATER RESOURCES

Clean, fresh water is vital to life, but droughts will make it scarce in regions that are already semideserts. Shrinking glaciers could have the same effect, because large areas of central Asia and China rely on water stored in the mountain glaciers of the Himalayas. Many South American cities such as Lima in Peru depend on the glaciers of the Andes in the same way. If the glaciers melt, the water that they contain will drain away. Flooding by rising sea levels could also contaminate the water supplies of some of the world's largest cities, which are built on low-lying coasts.

Wheat crops could benefit from warmer climates

FARM CROPS

Global warming could make farming harder in tropical countries, because many crops are grown in regions that are already as warm as the plants can stand. In temperate regions, cereal crops such as wheat may benefit from the longer summers and the higher levels of carbon dioxide, although this could be offset by increased ground-level ozone reducing plant growth.

FOOD SUPPLY

If farming in the tropics is badly hit by climate change, food supplies could start to dry up. This will have the biggest impact on people in developing countries who are already struggling to get enough to eat. It will affect other people too, all over the world. A lot of the food that is sold in our stores comes from the tropics. If local farmers cannot produce enough to make up for reduced supplies, the supermarket shelves will start to empty much faster.

BREAKDOWN

Developed countries rely on a network of services such as power, communications, and transportation to provide the necessities of life including food, water, and heating. This makes them just as vulnerable to destructive events as less complex societies. This was demonstrated by the chaos that followed the flooding of New Orleans by Hurricane Katrina in 2005, shown here from the air. While the service networks collapsed and many people lost their lives, the city sank into lawlessness, with looters stealing from damaged buildings and violent gangs roaming the streets.

Adapting to climate change

WE HAVE TO COMBAT CLIMATE CHANGE if we are to reduce the risk of catastrophic events in the future. Yet whatever we do, some change is inevitable. Even if we stopped all greenhouse gas emissions tomorrow, the average global temperature would still keep rising for the next 30 years, mainly because of the gradual release of heat stored by the oceans. The rising temperatures are bound to raise sea levels. They may also cause more droughts and floods, and create problems for agriculture and wildlife. So we must prepare for these changes, while working hard to stop the problem from getting worse.

TIDAL DEFENSES
Many great cities are built on low-lying coasts that are vulnerable to rising sea levels. Most of these cities already have sea defenses, but they will need extra protection against extra-high tides and storm surges. Some barriers have already been built. One of the largest, the Thames Barrier, was built in 1974–1982 to protect London, England, from storm surges that were already seen as a threat. The ten giant steel gates were used quite rarely until 1990, but as sea levels creep up, they have been closed a lot more often.

NATURAL BARRIERS
Developing nations often cannot afford to build coastal defenses, but the sea naturally creates barriers to storm waves in the form of shoals, salt marshes and, in warmer regions, mangrove swamps like this one in Florida. Many of these natural barriers have been destroyed by poorly planned coastal development. By preventing this, even poor countries can protect their coasts from flooding.

WILDLIFE RESERVES
Wildlife is already suffering from the massive destruction of habitats all over the world, and the extra stress of changing climates will drive many species into extinction. By creating wildlife reserves, we can make life easier for plants and animals, and also preserve the ecosystems that help resist serious climate change. This scientist is using computer technology to study plant growth in a tropical forest reserve in Costa Rica.

BATTLING THE DESERTS

People living on the fringes of expanding deserts can stop the sand from taking over by stabilizing sand dunes with palm fronds, as here in Morocco, or by planting drought-resistant grasses and shrubs. They can also stop dry grassland from turning into desert by preventing overgrazing by farm animals.

NEW FARM CROPS

Scientists at the International Rice Research Institute in the Philippines are developing new rice plants that can grow well in dryer, warmer climates. These may help stop rice yields from dwindling as temperatures rise. Away from the tropics, farmers may switch to food crops such as corn that are more suited to hotter, drier summers—although predicting exactly which crops will do well in a constantly changing climate may not be easy.

Pylons stop the houses from floating away

LIVING WITH THE FLOODS

Rivers swell naturally after heavy rain, and may spill over their banks. In the past this created broad, flat flood plains. In many countries regular flooding is prevented by high riverbanks, and the flood plains have been built on. But more intense storms are making these houses more vulnerable to flooding. In the low-lying Netherlands, people are dealing with the problem by building houses that float. These houses by the Maas River have watertight basements that act like rafts, and can rise up to 18 ft (5.5 m) on rising floodwaters.

SAFE REFUGES

Bangladesh is a very flat, low-lying land that suffers regular flooding as the Ganges and other rivers burst their banks after heavy monsoon rains. The local people have adapted by building mounds that rise above the flat landscape and provide refuges, both for them and their valuable cattle. When the floods drain away, the people and their animals can move back onto the surrounding land.

Metal buildings provide temporary shelter for the farmers

SOAKING UP STORMS

In many cities most of the ground is covered by concrete, so it cannot absorb heavy rain. The water spills down streets and overloads drainage systems, creating floods of stormwater and sewage. Parks and other green spaces—this is Central Park in New York —soak up rainwater and help prevent such flooding.

Combating climate change

CLIMATE CAMPAIGNS
Since the dangers of climate change were first recognized, ordinary people all over the world have campaigned for urgent action by governments. They have written to political leaders, signed petitions, given financial support to pressure groups, and staged mass protests and marches like this one in London in 2006.

WE MUST STOP GLOBAL temperatures from rising to the point where they cause dramatic, dangerous climate change. Since climate change is a global problem, it requires global action, but getting all the nations to agree on solutions is very difficult. This is partly because developed nations rely on the technologies that are causing the problem. They could have a lot to lose by replacing them, but they may have more to lose by risking climate chaos. New, less damaging technologies also provide opportunities for scientific innovation and wealth creation. So gradually, agreements are being forged to combat climate change.

IN THE MEDIA
As the scientific evidence for climate change has piled up, many media figures have joined or started climate campaigns. They range from music and movie stars to Al Gore, former vice-president of the United States and joint winner of the 2007 Nobel Peace Prize with the IPCC. He is seen here at the premiere of his 2006 film about global warming, *An Inconvenient Truth*.

FIGHTING BACK
The people who have most to lose from a move away from fossil fuels are the employees of the industries that profit from them. Accordingly in the 1990s, several oil companies formed the "Global Climate Coalition" to obstruct action to combat climate change. But the evidence is now so strong that some oil companies such as BP are funding research into alternative energy, as symbolized by this flower logo.

In 2000 BP changed its logo to a flower symbol

THE IPCC
In 1988 the United Nations asked for a high-level scientific assessment of the evidence for climate change. This led to the creation of the Intergovernmental Panel on Climate Change, or IPCC. Its role is to look at all the climate research carried out worldwide, and produce regular, detailed assessments of the scientists' conclusions. The first of these "assessment reports" was released in 1990, and it was followed by updated reports in 1995, 2001, and 2007. Here Bert Metz, co-chairman of one of the IPCC working groups, displays a report during a press conference in 2007.

Bert METZ
Co-chair IPCC Working Group III

SETTING A TARGET
At a meeting called "Avoiding Dangerous Climate Change" held in the UK in 2005, scientists agreed that if the average global temperature rises to more than 3.6°F (2°C) above its pre-industrial level, this could trigger catastrophic climate change. If nothing is done, we are likely to reach this point by 2050, so experts agree that we must cut global greenhouse gas emissions by 60 percent by 2050. This graph shows how carbon dioxide emissions could increase if we do nothing, and the reduction targets needed.

Graph: CO$_2$ emissions per year (Gt) versus Year (2000–2100)
- Average predicted CO$_2$ emissions without reduction
- Target CO$_2$ emissions reduction

THE KYOTO PROTOCOL
The world made a start on greenhouse gas reduction in 1997 at a meeting in Kyoto, Japan. Representatives of many countries, as seen above, agreed to aim for a global average reduction of roughly five percent by 2012. This has focused attention on the problem, but a much greater average cut in emissions will be needed in the future.

CARBON TRADING
Under the Kyoto Protocol—and other international agreements to reduce greenhouse gas emissions—countries that cannot meet their reduction targets have to buy "carbon credits" from nations with very low carbon emissions. It sounds like buying a licence to release greenhouse gases, but the total emissions of both nations cannot exceed their combined quotas. High-carbon nations can also fund projects in low-carbon nations, such as restoring forests using native trees like this seedling teak.

AN EQUAL SHARE
This shanty town in Lima, Peru, shows how many people live in cities in developing countries. It is only fair that they should have better living standards, but by improving their lives, they will almost certainly generate more greenhouse gases. To compensate for this, rich nations with high living standards would have to cut their greenhouse gas emissions by more than the global average of 60 percent required by 2050. A country like the US might have to cut its emissions by 80 percent or more—yet each US citizen would still be producing more carbon dioxide than each Peruvian. Many people hope that one day we will move toward a situation where everyone on the planet has a small but equal "carbon ration."

CARBON CUTBACK
Huge cutbacks in greenhouse gas emissions ranging from 60 to 80 percent might seem impossible, or only possible if we completely abandon our comfortable way of life. But by changing the way we generate power, the way we use energy in our homes, and the way we travel, we can make a big difference. Devices like this roadside carbon dioxide and pollution monitor are already focusing people's attention on what needs to be done.

Cutting the carbon

THE WORLD RELIES on electricity, but this has to be generated from other forms of energy. Currently most of it is produced by burning fossil fuels, which releases greenhouse gases. Luckily there are ways of reducing these emissions. Natural gas is cleaner than coal, so using it instead of coal can help. Converting coal into gas turns it into a more efficient fuel. Carbon dioxide can also be removed from fossil fuels before or after they are burned, and stored underground.

THE PRICE OF COAL
Even if coal could be burned cleanly, coal mining is dangerous and often destructive. Deep coal mines are notorious for deadly collapses and explosions. During 2006, when this photograph was taken in Sichuan, China, at least 5,986 Chinese workers were killed in mining accidents. Surface mines are safer, but they leave huge scars on the landscape.

THE COAL PROBLEM
Coal generates about two-thirds of the world's electricity. This is partly because it is a very abundant resource, especially in the United States and China. But burning coal produces far more carbon dioxide than using natural gas. Coal-fired power plants are also relatively inefficient, turning less than 40 percent of their fuel energy into electricity. Altogether, coal accounts for more than a quarter of global carbon dioxide emissions. Yet the US is likely to burn 40 percent more coal by 2025, and China intends to triple the energy that it produces from coal by 2020.

CARBON CAPTURE AND STORAGE

One way of cleaning up coal-fired power plants is by bubbling their exhaust gases through chemicals called ethanolamines, which absorb 82 to 99 percent of the carbon dioxide. The chemicals are piped away and heated to release the gas, which is collected and pumped underground for storage in old oil wells, coal mines, and reserves of salty water call saline aquifers. The carbon dioxide can also be used to help force oil out of oilfields, and to displace methane from old coal mines so that it can be used as a fuel. In theory, this technology could be used to virtually eliminate the carbon emissions from coal-fired power plants, and it is already being used in many countries.

Power Station

Oil rig

CO_2

CO_2

CO_2

Methane

Coal

Saline aquifer

Oil

9. Gas is used to generate electricity

1. Gasifier plant pumps air and steam underground

7. Carbon dioxide stripped from harvested gas

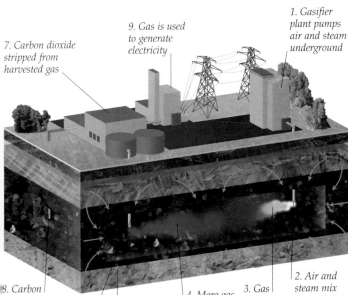

8. Carbon dioxide stored underground in depleted coal seams

6. Gas forced to surface up production well

5. Pressure of groundwater contains the gas

4. More gas is released from coal seam by heat

3. Gas mixture ignited to generate heat

2. Air and steam mix with gas from coal seam

UNDERGROUND COAL GASIFICATION

Instead of mining coal, it is possible to turn it into gas while it is still underground, and use the gas as a much more efficient fuel. Air and steam are pumped into a coal seam, which releases hydrogen, methane, and carbon dioxide. The gas mixture is ignited to generate heat, which turns more of the coal into gas. This is contained by the pressure of groundwater, and forced up a collection pipe to the surface. Here the carbon dioxide can be stripped out of the mixture and pumped back underground, and the gas can be used to generate electricity.

NATURAL GAS

Burning natural gas instead of coal to generate power releases about 40 percent less carbon doxide for each watt of electricity. It is also much cleaner in other ways, since it does not produce soot or sulfur compounds. So although gas is a fossil fuel, simply switching from coal to gas can dramatically reduce carbon dioxide emissions. However, the unburned gas is mostly methane, which is a far more powerful greenhouse gas than carbon dioxide. So any gas leaks, perhaps from pipelines like this one in Canada, can wipe out any advantage that gas has over coal.

Model of an LNG tanker

LIQUID FUEL

Natural gas can now be shipped all over the world in special gas tankers that transport it as liquefied natural gas (LNG). The liquefying process uses energy, making LNG up to 30 percent less efficient as a fuel than ordinary natural gas—but it is much more efficient than coal. LNG is highly explosive, so finding suitable sites for gas terminals can be a problem. Since many of the world's gas reserves are now almost exhausted, carrying gas around the globe in LNG tankers may soon be essential if we are to avoid relying on coal.

Nuclear power

THERE IS ONE POWERFUL, reliable energy source that, when it is up and running, emits no greenhouse gases at all. Nuclear fission exploits the colossal amount of energy released by radioactive uranium when its atoms are split in a nuclear reactor. But radiation is extremely dangerous, and since a reactor can also be used to make nuclear weapons, nuclear power is the subject of fierce debate between those who support this form of energy generation and those who oppose it.

NUCLEAR FISSION

A single atom of uranium is unbelievably small, but it can be made to yield a huge amount of energy by splitting the nucleus at its heart into two smaller parts. This can be done by hitting it with a tiny particle called a neutron. As each atomic nucleus splits, it releases energy and more neutrons. These split more nuclei in a chain reaction. If this is not controlled, it can cause a nuclear explosion, but if it takes place in a carefully designed nuclear reactor, it just generates a lot of heat.

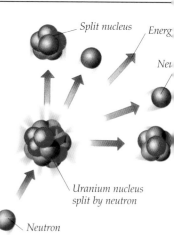

Split nucleus
Energy
Neu
Uranium nucleus split by neutron
Neutron

NUCLEAR POWER PLANT

This nuclear power plant in England has two nuclear reactors. Each one contains rods of radioactive uranium that interact in a nuclear chain reaction. The reaction is regulated by "control rods" that are lowered between the radioactive fuel rods to absorb neutrons and stop the rods from interacting. The heat generated by the nuclear reaction heats a fluid that is pumped through a boiler to turn water into steam. This powers turbines linked to electricity generators.

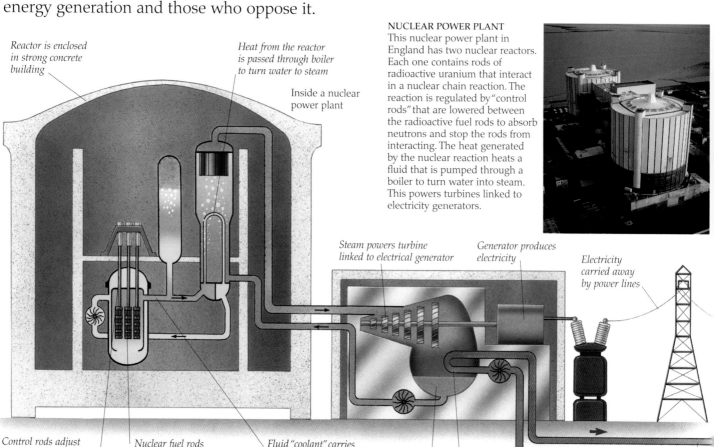

Reactor is enclosed in strong concrete building

Heat from the reactor is passed through boiler to turn water to steam

Inside a nuclear power plant

Steam powers turbine linked to electrical generator

Generator produces electricity

Electricity carried away by power lines

Control rods adjust rate of nuclear reaction

Nuclear fuel rods generate heat in reactor

Fluid "coolant" carries heat away from reactor

Cooled steam forms water, which is pumped back to boiler

Steam cooled by cold water

Cooled water returns from cooling tower

Hot water flows to cooling tower

CARBON-FREE POWER

Nearly 80 percent of France's electricity is generated by nuclear energy. It powers France's famous high-speed train, or Train à Grande Vitesse (TGV), which covers long distances at up to 186 mph (300 km/h), rivaling aircraft for speed, but with zero carbon emissions. This gives France a relatively low "carbon footprint" in relation to its wealth and industrial productivity. However, although many other nations would like to follow France's example, nuclear power stations are very expensive and take a long time to build. Setting up an entire network can take ten years or more.

RADIOACTIVE WASTE

A nuclear power station uses a tiny quantity of nuclear fuel, but after it has been used, it remains highly radioactive for thousands of years. This is a serious problem, because the radiation is very dangerous to health. The waste must be handled by remote control and stored in special facilities while scientists try to find ways of making it safe. Here spent nuclear fuel is stored in a tank of water, which stops the radiation from escaping.

NUCLEAR WEAPONS

As well as generating power, nuclear reactors can be adapted to make nuclear bombs capable of destroying entire cities. If nuclear power becomes widely used, more countries may develop nuclear weapons, and possibly use them to threaten or even destroy their enemies. Radioactive material might also be stolen by terrorists, who could pack it around ordinary explosives to make "dirty bombs" that could spread dangerously radioactive dust.

Australian uranium mine

URANIUM MINING

Uranium—the radioactive metal used as nuclear fuel—is a rare metal that may be in short supply within a few decades. Mining it uses a lot of conventional energy that generates greenhouse gases, as does the construction of a nuclear power plant, so nuclear power is not entirely carbon-neutral. The mines also leave huge scars in the landscape.

NUCLEAR ACCIDENTS

In 1986 the Chernobyl reactor near Kiev in Ukraine overheated and blew up. Radioactive dust spread over a large area of the former USSR, and some was even carried around the world by the wind. Many people died of radiation poisoning, including a lot of the workers seen here trying to clear up the contamination. Many more will probably suffer cancers triggered by the radiation. The Chernobyl plant was a primitive, badly-run reactor, and modern nuclear power stations are far safer, yet many people worry that other nuclear power plants could explode. They also fear that nuclear plants could become terrorist targets.

Hydrogen nucleus with one neutron (deuterium)

Hydrogen nucleus with two neutrons (tritium)

Nuclei collide and fuse

NUCLEAR FUSION

If small atomic nuclei are smashed together, they can fuse together to make bigger nuclei. This is the opposite of nuclear fission, but it also produces huge amounts of energy. All the energy radiated by the Sun is generated by this nuclear fusion process. It does not involve radioactive fuel, and it does not create radioactive waste. But it does require a colossal input of energy to get it started, and controlling the process is very difficult. Experimental fusion reactors are now being tested at several laboratories around the world, but it will be a very long time before nuclear fusion is used to generate electricity.

Energy

Helium nucleus forms

Neutron released

Renewable energy

FOR CENTURIES PEOPLE have been harnessing the energy of wind and flowing water to power windmills and watermills. This technology has now been updated to drive electricity generators. Solar energy and even volcanic heat can also be turned into electricity. Such energy sources are described as renewable because they never run out. They may not be able to provide all our energy needs, but most of them do not release any of the greenhouse gases that are causing climate change.

HYDROELECTRIC POWER
Rainwater flowing off the land can be used to power turbines linked to electricity generators. To ensure a steady flow, the water is stored in reservoirs created by building huge dams across upland river valleys. This means that the power plants can be built only in suitable terrain. The dams can cause serious problems for wildlife, and the reservoirs often silt up. But hydroelectric power is a proven, dependable technology that currently supplies 15 percent of the world's electricity.

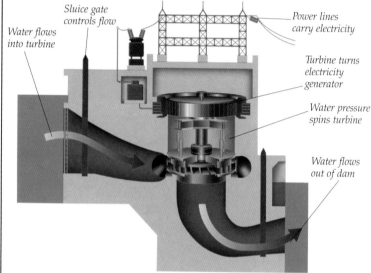

Sluice gate controls flow

Water flows into turbine

Power lines carry electricity

Turbine turns electricity generator

Water pressure spins turbine

Water flows out of dam

WATER PRESSURE
A hydroelectric scheme relies on the immense water pressure created by having a colossal weight of water trapped behind the dam. The water pressure spins the blades of huge turbines that are built into tunnels passing through the dam, and these turbines turn the generators that produce electricity. The water flow can be controlled and even stopped completely by sluice gates in the tunnels. This allows the output of the power plant to be matched to demand and water supply. Stopping the flow also enables engineers to maintain the turbines and other machinery.

WAVES AND OCEAN CURRENTS
Several power plants that harness wave energy have been built, but they work well only on exposed sites that can rely on big waves throughout the year. More promising schemes involve exploiting ocean currents. The picture below shows how giant submarine turbines might be used to generate power from the fast-flowing Gulf Stream near the Bahamas. It is estimated that a scheme like this could produce as much electricity as a nuclear power plant.

TIDAL BARRAGES
A hydroelectric dam can be built across a tidal inlet on the coast. Gates in the dam open to allow water in as the tide rises every day. At high tide the gates are closed, and as the tide falls again, the water behind the barrage is allowed out through turbines linked to electricity generators. Some systems like this tidal plant in France exploit both the incoming and outgoing tide. Tidal barrages produce clean electricity, but they can be extremely damaging to coastal wildlife habitats because they disrupt or even prevent the natural ebb and flow of the tides.

Huge rotors drive waterproofed electricity generators

WIND FARMS

Wind is already being harnessed on a large scale by "wind farms" of hi-tech wind turbines. Many are sited on land, often in hilly, scenic regions where people resent their impact on the landscape. Offshore wind farms such as this one near Copenhagen, Denmark, experience stronger, more consistent winds and they can be built well away from land, although there are concerns about seabirds being killed by the huge rotors. The main practical problem is that wind turbines work only when the wind blows. This means that there must be back-up power generation systems, which often have to use fossil fuels.

GEOTHERMAL ENERGY

In volcanic regions, energy can be tapped from hot rock and water beneath the ground. It can be used directly to heat water and houses, as in Iceland where it heats 90 percent of the buildings. The heat can also run the turbines of power stations like this one at Wairakei, New Zealand. Geothermal power in California, Mexico, Indonesia, Italy, and Iceland is producing as much electricity as about ten large coal-fired power plants, but it could be used far more widely, wherever there is volcanic activity.

SOLAR POWER PLANTS

Most solar power systems are small-scale, but a few big power plants have been built in reliably sunny regions such as California and Spain. They use mirrors to focus the Sun's rays on a tower that collects the heat and uses it to run a turbine and generator. More efficient power lines may enable such plants to distribute power to cities in less sunny areas.

Cut sugar cane

Crop of sugar cane

BIOFUEL CROPS

Burning any plant product as a fuel releases carbon dioxide. However, if more plants are grown to replace them when they are harvested, the new crop should absorb the carbon dioxide that is released. Some of these crops can be used as fuel in their raw state, but plants such as switchgrass and sugarcane are converted into fuel oils and ethanol. However, growing enough biofuels to replace all the fossil fuels that we rely on would use up all the farmland that we now use to grow food, or require massive deforestation. It would also generate greenhouse gases through the use of fertilizers and machinery.

Power for the people

SOLAR HOT WATER
Solar energy is free, abundant, and non-polluting. The most efficient way to use it on a small scale is for heating the water we use for bathing and washing. Many systems use roof panels made of copper pipes in glass tubes. Sunlight passing through the glass heats fluid pumped through the pipes, and the hot fluid heats the water. A conventional boiler can act as back-up in winter, but in summer the Sun can supply enough energy to raise the water temperature to more than 140°F (60°C).

BIG POWER PLANTS GENERATING megawatts of electricity are essential for keeping large-scale infrastructure running, but households and small communities can provide some or even all of their own power without using fossil fuels. Some is in the form of electricity, and some in the form of heat energy. A lot of the technology used to produce this local power is still being perfected— it is not as efficient as it might be, and it can cost a lot. But its efficiency will improve, and as more people start using devices such as solar panels and heat pumps, they will get a lot less expensive. Soon they will be as common as satellite TV.

WOOD-BURNING STOVES
Burning wood or similar plant products in a solid-fuel stove to provide heat can be carbon-neutral, if the carbon dioxide that it releases is absorbed by the growth of new fuel plants. Fuel can also be made from waste wood, and from other waste products such as cardboard and paper that might otherwise be buried in landfill sites. But such "biomass" fuels are only suitable for small-scale use, because growing enough of them to fuel a city would use up far too much land.

SOLAR ELECTRICITY
Some solar panels generate electricity. These are built up from many solar photovoltaic (solar PV) elements that convert light into electrical energy. They work best in sunny places like the southern United States, where they can run the air-conditioning systems that use most power when the sun is shining strongly. In the developing world, solar panels linked to batteries provide lighting for households that would otherwise rely on oil lamps. Here the clear skies over Central Asia allow a small solar array to power the TV of a Mongolian family—linked to a huge satellite dish that almost dwarfs their traditional home.

WIND TURBINES

For decades sailors have used wind generators to recharge the batteries on their boats. Similar technology can produce electrical power for houses, although a small wind turbine like this would generate only a small fraction of the electricity used by a typical household. Larger turbines provide more power, but many houses are not built strongly enough to support them. More efficient turbines will eventually become available, however—and if people find ways of using less energy, local or domestic wind power will become a more viable option.

SIMPLE TECHNOLOGY

One advantage of small-scale power generation systems is that they can be easy to set up and maintain. Wind pumps such as the one shown here have been used to pump water for centuries, because they are simple and reliable, and can be repaired without specialist knowledge and equipment. Small power generators are more complex, but many can still be maintained by the people who use them. This makes them ideal for use in developing countries, and by people who live in remote regions. They also allow people to live comfortably without relying on national grid networks, which can be valuable if conventional power supplies fail.

HOME HYDROELECTRICITY

People who have access to streams—especially fast-flowing upland streams—can sometimes harness their power to provide free, reliable electricity without generating any greenhouse gases. These small hydro-electric systems typically use small turbines rather than large wheels of the type once used by watermills. But they do rely on a good "head of water" to build up enough water pressure and keep the turbine running during dry weather, and this often involves creating the modern equivalent of a millpond. Very few people have enough space, even if they have the water.

Insulated roof keeps in the heat

Underfloor heating system

Pump and heat exchanger

Fluid is pumped through underground coil

Heated fluid returning to house

Fluid is heated by warm ground

GROUND-SOURCE HEAT PUMPS

In winter, the temperature below ground stays higher than that of the air above. The heat can be collected using a long coil of pipe containing water and antifreeze, buried in a garden or beneath a house. The warmed fluid passes through a heat-exchanger linked to an underfloor heating system, and although it needs an electric pump, the technique generates up to four times the energy it uses. There are already about 600,000 ground-source heat pumps working in the United States.

Energy efficiency

SUPPLYING POWER without using the fossil fuels that contribute to climate change is not easy. Wind farms, for example, produce far less electricity than fuel-burning power plants, and the wind does not blow all the time. But if we all used less energy, technologies such as wind and solar power would be able to cope with a bigger proportion of the demand. We can help to achieve this by improving energy efficiency, or making sure things use less power to do the same job. This applies both to the people who design equipment, and to the people who use it.

ENERGY RATING
Some home equipment such as fridges must be left on all the time, and others such as washing machines may run for many hours a day. They can waste a lot of energy if they work inefficiently. New kitchen appliances in most parts of the world are now labeled with their efficiency rating, so people can avoid buying energy-wasting designs. These labels for a washing machine in New Zealand show its energy consumption and efficiency, as well as its water conservation rating.

WASTEFUL DESIGN
A lot of the electrical devices that we buy have been designed without considering the energy that they use. Anything that has a separate power supply plugged into a power socket uses power all the time —even if it is not in use—unless the power supply is switched off at the wall. Many gadgets are designed never to be switched off, like DVD recorders and digital TV receivers with built-in clocks and tuners. If they are unplugged they may need reprogramming, so they have to be left on "standby" all the time. Plasma-screen TVs like this one use almost five times as much energy as smaller traditional TVs, and 30–65 percent more energy than equally big LCD models.

EFFICIENT LIGHTING

Used in our houses since being invented by Thomas Edison in 1879, normal incandescent bulbs are highly inefficient. About five percent of the electricity used to power a standard 100-watt light bulb is actually converted into light—the other 95 percent is wasted as heat. Compact fluorescent "energy-saving" bulbs like this one produce about four times as much light per watt of electricity. Bulbs that use clusters of light-emitting diodes (LEDs) are even more efficient.

BUILDING STANDARDS

In winter many houses lose heat through their walls, windows, doors, roofs, and even through their floors—heat that is replaced by their heating systems using more energy. This infrared image shows heat escaping from a house as white and red, while the cooler areas are blue. Better design and building standards can help prevent this. New houses that meet the strict building standards in Sweden, for example, use roughly four times less energy than many older houses in the UK.

STORES AND OFFICES

Vast amounts of energy are wasted in stores and offices. Big food stores have rows of open fridges that spill cold air. Office lights and computers are often left running all night. By contrast, the Swiss Re Tower in London is designed to save energy. This building's shape minimizes the cooling effects of the wind and maximizes natural light, reducing the use of heating and lighting.

ECO-HOUSES

There are ways of building homes that use virtually no energy at all for heating or air-conditioning. They are naturally warmer in winter and cooler in summer, thanks to very efficient wall and roof insulation, and triple-glazed windows that make the most of natural light energy. This European housing scheme is also designed to use only energy from renewable sources, generated by solar panels and a local combined heat and power plant fueled by waste products.

ECO-CITIES

Whole communities have been converted or designed with energy-saving as a priority. They include Freiburg in Germany, which has some 6,500 energy-efficient homes incorporating solar technology. The new city of Dongtan on Chongmin Island off Shanghai, China, is being built from the ground up as the world's first "eco-city," with renewable power from its own wind farm. This artist's impression by Arup, the project managers, shows the proposed South Village area.

Green transportation

THE TRANSPORT OF PEOPLE and freight accounts for at least 14 percent of global greenhouse gas emissions. This figure is increasing, especially in many developing nations. Technology may help through the development of more efficient vehicles, powered by less polluting fuels. But most of the more exciting proposals are still at the design stage, and some may not work in practice. So in the short term, the best way to reduce greenhouse gas emissions from transportation is to change the way we travel, and not travel so much.

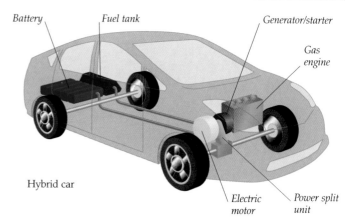

Hybrid car

Battery — Fuel tank — Generator/starter — Gas engine — Electric motor — Power split unit

ELECTRIC CARS AND HYBRIDS
Electric cars are less polluting than normal cars, but they cannot travel far and take a long time to recharge. One solution is the hybrid, which has a small engine linked to a generator that charges a battery. This drives an electric motor that can boost the power of the engine through a "power split" device. Since the electrical power is used only when needed, the car produces less carbon dioxide than conventional cars.

Strong frame forms safety cage

Lightweight materials reduce emissions

CAR DESIGN
Car engines are more efficient than they used to be, and produce fewer greenhouse gases in relation to their power. But most cars are much heavier and faster than they were before, so they need bigger, more powerful engines that use more fuel. Many manufacturers are fighting the trend by producing small, lightweight vehicles like the Smart Car shown above. These produce far fewer greenhouse gases, because they can be powered by small engines.

Container holds used cooking oil from restaurants

RECYCLED FUELS
Most cars run on fossil fuels, but they can also use renewable fuels made from plants. Gasoline engines can burn a small percentage of ethanol, an alcohol made from plant material, and diesel engines can use "biodiesel" made from crops such as sunflowers or soya. Growing crops to make fuel can do more harm than good, but diesel engines can be modified to use recycled cooking oil, which would otherwise be thrown away. The oil can be cleaned up using a home refinery like this.

HYDROGEN

Hydrogen gas could be the ultimate clean fuel, because when it is mixed with oxygen and burned, it produces only energy and water vapour, which can be condensed into liquid water to prevent it becoming a greenhouse gas. Hydrogen can also be made from water, but the process uses a lot of electrical energy. The gas cannot be carried in a normal fuel tank unless it is turned into a liquid by chilling it to the amazingly low temperature of −253°C (−423°F). Despite this, hydrogen-powered vehicles like this bus are being tested, mostly based on "fuel cells" that use the hydrogen to produce electricity that powers electric motors.

BIOFUELS

Biofuels may be carbon neutral in themselves, but growing biofuel crops like these oil palms is already leading to the destruction of tropical rain forests. Growing the crops also releases nitrous oxide, an extremely powerful greenhouse gas. So using biofuels instead of fossil fuels can actually increase greenhouse gas emissions, by up to several hundred percent.

PUBLIC TRANSPORTATION

People who live in big cities routinely use buses, trains, and trams like these in the streets of Amsterdam in the Netherlands. These public transportation systems use energy much more efficiently than cars because they carry a lot of passengers, and often employ more efficient technology such as electric power. In rural areas, public transportation is less popular because the services are less frequent, so many people use cars. But rising fuel prices and road congestion could encourage more people to use public transportation in the future, and the services may improve as a result.

PEDAL POWER

Over short distances, bikes are quicker than cars, and the only greenhouse gas they release is the carbon dioxide in the breath of their riders. Beijing in China, seen here during the morning rush-hour, is famous for its crowds of cyclists. Many other cities also encourage cycling, and cars are virtually banned from some downtowns. The result is a much cleaner, safer, friendlier environment, and far fewer greenhouse gas emissions.

AIR TRAVEL

Every flight by a jet aircraft ejects a huge amount of carbon dioxide and other emissions at high altitude, in the most vulnerable part of the atmosphere. Propeller-driven aircraft are less polluting, but they are also much slower. Alternative fuels are being investigated, but they are unlikely to help. However, bigger, more fuel-efficient aircraft such as this Airbus A380 may enable airlines to control greenhouse gas emissions— if air travel stays at current levels.

Your carbon footprint

YOU CAN HELP DEFEAT CLIMATE CHANGE by reducing your carbon footprint. This is the amount of carbon dioxide, or its equivalent in other greenhouse gases, released as a result of the things you do. It is the mark you make upon the planet—and the smaller it is, the better. Even little things make a difference if we all do them. Many have no effect on our lives except to save money, like switching off the light when leaving a room. Other decisions are harder, like avoiding flying or using public transportation instead of the car. One day we may have "carbon rationing" in which everyone gets a fair share of humanity's total carbon footprint. If this happens, we can each decide how to use our share. Until then, your wasteful neighbors may make your own efforts seem pointless. Do not let this put you off. Your planet needs you.

SWITCH IT OFF
Huge amounts of greenhouse gas are created by people leaving electronic equipment switched on for no reason. Many gadgets have a "standby" mode which makes them look as if they are off when they are actually using power. The mains adaptors that power or charge small electronic devices also use power if left plugged in. If you can switch off unused equipment at the wall without affecting the data stored in its memory, then do it.

TURN IT DOWN
Central heating is controlled by a thermostat, which switches it off when the room warms up. Turning down the thermostat by just 1.8°F (1°C) saves 518 lb (235 kg) of carbon dioxide emissions per year. Have a family discussion about it. Aim for 61–64°F (16–18°C); if you're a bit cold, wear more clothes.

USE YOUR LEGS
Cars are responsible for a lot of the greenhouse gas emissions that are causing climate change, so try to avoid using them. In particular, avoid asking to be taken on short car trips, because they use a lot more fuel per mile than long ones. Walk or use a bike, if the roads are safe. It will get you in shape, and can be a lot of fun. Catch a bus or a train for longer trips. Many public transportation companies offer discounts for young passengers that can make this a cheaper option than car travel. If the car is the only option, share it, or get a lift with a friend.

Vegetarian pizza is tasty, healthy, and better for the planet

THINK ABOUT WHAT YOU EAT
A meat-rich diet adds to greenhouse gas emissions, because raising animals such as cattle adds a lot of methane to the atmosphere. Some of the meat that we buy is imported from far away, which uses fossil fuels and increases emissions. Some of it comes from places where rain forest has been cleared to provide grazing land for beef cattle. It has been calculated that every mouthful of beef that we eat represents the emission of 6,800 times its own weight in greenhouse gases.

RE-USE AND RECYCLE
Our habit of throwing things away contributes to climate change by adding to methane-generating landfill. It also encourages us to buy new things that have been made using processes that emit greenhouse gases. Try to use things for as long as possible, getting them repaired if necessary. If they cannot be repaired, try to get them recycled rather than simply dumping them. This applies to everything from bottles and shopping bags to broken computers and TVs.

Recycling bins take all kinds of waste

BUY LOCAL
Get your family to support your local stores and markets, by making shopping expeditions on foot or by local bus rather than in the car. Avoid buying foods that have traveled halfway around the globe, if there are perfectly good alternatives from local sources. There is nothing wrong with a few exotic treats, but there is no point in buying air-freighted fruit when the same crop is being harvested locally. Get into the habit of checking the "country of origin" labels—and avoid buying things that come with a lot of packaging.

TAKE THE TRAIN
Avoid short-haul flights. A flight from London to Paris releases 538 lb (244 kg) of carbon dioxide per passenger, but a high-speed train trip between the same cities releases 48 lb (22 kg) per passenger. This particular trip is also quicker by train from downtown to downtown. If you are traveling further, you may have to take a flight, but ask your family to investigate "carbon offsetting" schemes, which aim to balance the plane's emissions by saving greenhouse gases elsewhere.

GROW A TREE
If you get the opportunity, plant a tree—preferably a native one that will provide a home for local wildlife. Even more importantly, make sure the tree keeps growing. Plant it in a place where it can grow to full maturity, and keep it watered when it is young. It will take a long time to grow big enough to absorb a lot of carbon dioxide from the atmosphere, but even a single tree could offset a lot of the greenhouse gases you will produce in your lifetime. If you cannot grow your own tree, support a forest charity that will grow one for you.

Greenhouse gas producers

CLIMATE CHANGE IS BEING CAUSED by humanity adding greenhouse gases to the atmosphere. These absorb heat radiated by Earth, and stop it from escaping out into space. There are several of these gases, and they come from various sources. Some nations release a lot more than others, partly because they are larger, but also because most of their citizens are richer and have a bigger carbon footprint.

EMISSIONS BY SECTOR

Most of the gases that are adding to the greenhouse effect are released by natural processes such as organic decay and the breathing of people and animals. However, the gases are also being generated by human activities. Many of these involve the rapid burning of fossil fuels. There are eight main sectors responsible for greenhouse gas emissions. Currently the biggest is the generation of electricity by power plants that burn fossil fuel, but emissions from transportation are growing rapidly. The picture could change dramatically in the future, especially if the destruction of tropical forests continues, or the global use of fossil fuels is radically reduced.

Power stations
21.7%

Industrial processes
16.8%

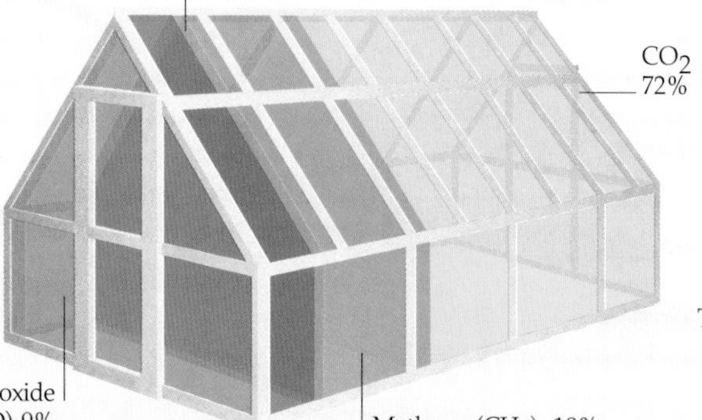

Transportation fuels 14.0%

Agricultural byproducts
12.5%

Fossil fuel extraction, processing, and distribution
11.3%

Waste disposal and treatment
3.4%

Residential and commercial
10.3%

Land use and biomass burning
10.0%

Artificial gases (CFCs, HFCs, PFCs, and SF6) 1%

CO_2
72%

Industrial processes
20.6%

Power stations
29.8%

Transportation fuels 19.2%

Fossil fuel extraction, processing, and distribution 8.4%

Nitrous oxide (N_2O) 9%

Methane (CH_4) 18%

Residential and commercial
12.9%

Land use and biomass burning 9.1%

GREENHOUSE GAS EMISSIONS BY WEIGHT

A number of gases released through human activity are increasing the power of the greenhouse effect. This diagram shows the relative quantities of the major human-produced greenhouse gases. The most important is carbon dioxide, because so much of it is released every year. The other greenhouse gases are emitted in smaller quantities, but they have a big effect because they are more powerful than carbon dioxide.

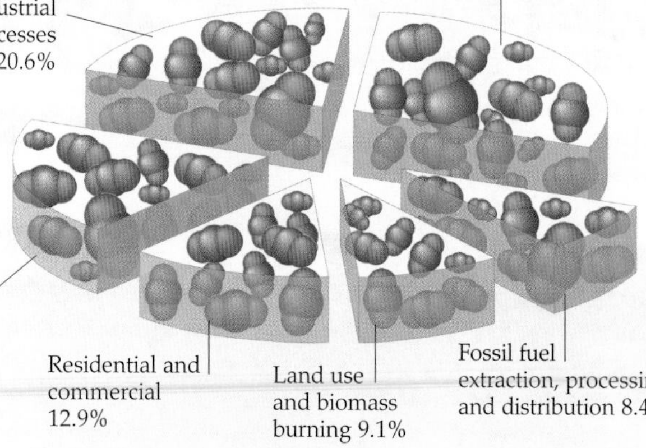

CARBON DIOXIDE BY SECTOR

Of all the greenhouse gases that we are releasing, carbon dioxide is currently having the most impact on the climate. Most of it is being emitted from power plants that burn coal or natural gas, but a lot is released by industry and transportation. The land use sector includes the felling and burning of forests.

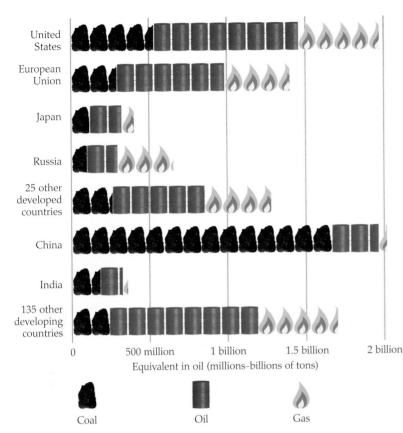

United States
European Union
Japan
Russia
25 other developed countries
China
India
135 other developing countries

| 0 | 500 million | 1 billion | 1.5 billion | 2 billion |

Equivalent in oil (millions–billions of tons)

Coal   Oil   Gas

FOSSIL FUEL CONSUMPTION

The main source of all the extra carbon dioxide in the atmosphere is the burning of fossil fuels. These include coal, oil in all its refined forms, and natural gas. All these fuels contain a lot of carbon. This chart shows that the annual consumption of fossil fuels varies by region and by country. The biggest consumers of fossil fuels are the United States, China, and the European Union. Coal produces far more carbon dioxide per unit of energy than the other fuels, so countries that burn a lot of coal, such as China, have a bigger impact on the climate than countries that burn more gas.

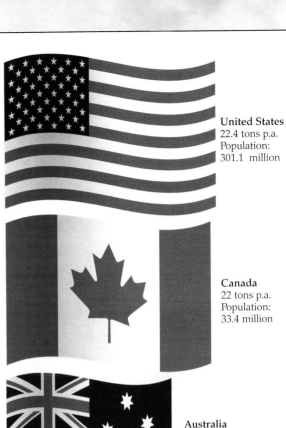

United States
22.4 tons p.a.
Population:
301.1 million

Canada
22 tons p.a.
Population:
33.4 million

Australia
18 tons p.a.
Population:
20.4 million

Russia
11.5 tons p.a.
Population: 141.4 million

Japan
10.8 tons p.a.
Population: 127.4 million

United Kingdom
10.7 tons p.a.
Population: 60.8 million

France
6.8 tons p.a.
Population: 63.7 million

 **China**
4.2 tons p.a. Population: 1.3 billion

 **Brazil**
2 tons p.a. Population: 190 million

India
1.3 tons p.a. Population: 1.1 billion

CARBON DIOXIDE PER PERSON

The size of the flags above indicates the average amount of carbon dioxide released per annum (p.a.) by each citizen of a few selected nations. The flags show that, although China burns more fossil fuel than any other country, the average carbon footprint of each Chinese citizen is relatively small.

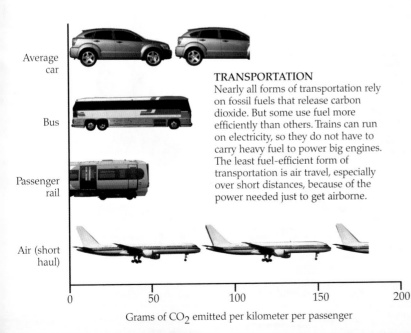

Average car

Bus

Passenger rail

Air (short haul)

TRANSPORTATION

Nearly all forms of transportation rely on fossil fuels that release carbon dioxide. But some use fuel more efficiently than others. Trains can run on electricity, so they do not have to carry heavy fuel to power big engines. The least fuel-efficient form of transportation is air travel, especially over short distances, because of the power needed just to get airborne.

| 0 | 50 | 100 | 150 | 200 |

Grams of CO_2 emitted per kilometer per passenger

Timeline

SCIENTISTS STUDY CHANGES in Earth's climate by analyzing rock formations, ice cores, and plant growth over millions of years. The first weather records started in the 18th century, and methods of measuring atmospheric changes have only been developed in the last 150 years. This timeline tracks the events that have had a significant effect on Earth's climate and the techniques used to study them.

Model of *Tyrannosaurus rex*, which became extinct 65 million years ago

250 MILLION YEARS AGO (MYA)
The biggest mass extinction in Earth's history destroys 96 percent of species living at the time. It is believed that massive volcanic eruptions released vast amounts of carbon dioxide that increased the greenhouse effect, causing serious global warming and making life on Earth almost impossible.

250–65 MYA
The globe experiences a warm, ice-free period that leads to the age of dinosaurs. This ends with another mass extinction, possibly caused by catastrophic volcanic activity coupled with the impact of a huge asteroid.

55 MYA
A long period of global cooling begins, eventually leading to the ice ages that peak about 20,000 years ago. We are currently living in a relatively warm phase of an ice age.

15,000 YEARS AGO
The last cold phase of the current ice age ends, and the vast ice sheets that cover much of North America, Europe, and northern Asia begin to melt.

13,000 YEARS AGO
Disruption of ocean currents caused by vast quantities of meltwater entering the north Atlantic cause a local temperature drop that lasts for 1,300 years. This is the period known as the "Younger Dryas."

8,000 YEARS AGO
Carbon dioxide levels in the atmosphere rise by about 8 percent, at a time when the first farmers were clearing and burning large areas of forest to create fields.

6,000 YEARS AGO
Drought brings an end to an 8,000-year monsoon climate in north Africa, turning tropical grasslands into the vast desert that we now know as the Sahara.

1000CE
Temperatures rise to the peak of the "Medieval Warm Period," when the climate was as warm as it is today. In Mexico a prolonged drought causes the abandonment of many Mayan cities.

1430
Europe enters a "Little Ice Age" that lasts until the 1800s. The low temperatures cause widespread crop failures and famines, and make rivers and canals freeze over each winter. The cool period may have been linked to increased volcanic activity producing ash clouds that partly reflected the Sun's rays.

Industrial use of coal begins in 1709

1607
The first Frost Fair is held on the frozen Thames River in London. Tents, sideshows, and food stalls are erected on the thick ice. The last Frost Fair is held in 1813, toward the end of the Little Ice Age.

1703
Britain's most severe storm on record, known as the Great Storm, destroys many towns and kills 123 people on land, 8,000 at sea.

1709
British industrialist Abraham Darby invents a way of using coal to produce iron, and this begins the intense use of fossil fuels as an industrial energy source. The resulting Industrial Revolution is marked by a rise in the level of atmospheric carbon dioxide.

1807
Coal gas provides the fuel for the first street lighting scheme in London.

1815
The Indonesian volcano Tambora explodes in the largest volcanic eruption in recorded history. Airborne ash shading Earth causes the "year without a summer" of 1816.

1827
French mathematician Jean Baptiste Fourier discovers the greenhouse effect, by which gases in the atmosphere trap heat radiated from the Sun-warmed Earth.

1840
Swiss-born scientist Louis Agassiz proposes his theory of ice ages, and realizes that northern Europe was once covered by an ice sheet.

1847
The world's first oil well is drilled at Baku in Azerbaijan.

1856
The first refinery for crude oil is set up at Ulaszowice in Poland.

1863
Irish scientist John Tyndall publishes a paper describing how water vapor can act as a greenhouse gas.

1882
American inventor Thomas Edison sets up the world's first commercial coal-fired electricity generating station—the Pearl Street plant in lower Manhattan, New York. It is used to supply power for the incandescent light bulbs invented by Edison in 1879.

1885
German engineer Karl Benz creates the first practical gasoline-engined car.

1895
Swedish chemist Svante Arrhenius suggests that adding carbon dioxide to the Earth's atmosphere by burning coal might increase the greenhouse effect, causing global warming.

Edison's light bulb, invented in 1879

1908
In the United States, the Model T Ford goes into mass production, and car ownership starts to rise rapidly.

1920
Serbian scientist Milutin Milankovitch discovers how regular variations in Earth's orbit around the Sun cause cycles of changing global temperature that are probably responsible for ice ages.

Mass production of Model T Ford starts in 1908

1931
After three years of drought, torrential rain falls for months in China. This causes the Yangtze River to flood catastrophically, rising up to 95 ft (29 m) above its usual level. As a result 3.7 million people die through disease, starvation, or drowning. It is the most destructive climatic event in history.

1932
Following years of drought, the desperately dry soil of the "Dust Bowl" in the American Midwest starts to blow away. The dust storms continue until 1939.

1939
British engineer Guy Stewart Callendar argues that observed global warming since the 1800s could be explained by a 10 percent rise in atmospheric carbon dioxide. He suggests that a doubling of carbon dioxide in the atmosphere would bring about an average global temperature increase of 3.6°F (2°C).

1945
After rising steadily for about a century, global temperatures start to fall slowly because air pollution by soot and other particles partly obscures the Sun.

1957
After discovering that the oceans cannot absorb all the extra carbon dioxide being created by the burning of fossil fuels, US oceanographer Roger Revelle warns that humanity is conducting a "large-scale geophysical experiment" by releasing greenhouse gases into the atmosphere.

1958
Charles Keeling starts recording atmospheric carbon dioxide concentrations, first in Antarctica, and then in Hawaii. Over the following years, he records a steady long-term rise with annual fluctuations caused by Northern Hemisphere winters. The graph's line is described as the "sawtoothed curve."

1962
Russian climate expert Mikhail Budyko warns that the exponential growth of industrial civilization could cause drastic global warming within the next century.

1967
US geophysicists Syukuro Manabe and Richard Wetherald devise an early computer model of the global climate. This agrees with Callendar's earlier suggestion that a doubling of atmospheric carbon dioxide could cause a global temperature rise of 3.6°F (2°C). Later computer models revise this figure to an even higher 5.4°F (3°C).

1968–74
The Sahel region on the southern fringes of the Sahara in Africa suffers a seven-year drought. Millions die of starvation, and by the end of the drought, 50 million people are relying on food aid for survival.

1970
The worst tropical storm of the 20th century occurs in Bangladesh, where flooding caused by a 25 ft (7.5 m) storm surge in the Bay of Bengal kills up to 500,000 people.

1976–77
Europe suffers a major drought, which in Britain is the worst for 250 years.

1977
Records show that global temperatures start to rise again after a reduction in soot emissions reduces the "global dimming" effect that air pollution is thought to have.

1982
Swiss physicist Hans Oeschger, working on atmospheric samples trapped in the ancient ice of the Greenland ice sheet, confirms the link between increasing atmospheric carbon dioxide and global warming.

1982–83
Eastern Australia suffers its worst drought of the 20th century. It triggers the disastrous "Ash Wednesday" fires that kill over 60 people around Victoria and Adelaide.

1984–85
A long drought in Ethiopia and Sudan kills 450,000 people.

1985
A drilling team at Vostok Station in central Antarctica produces an ice core that contains a 150,000-year record of temperature and atmospheric carbon dioxide. This "Vostok core" shows that the levels of both have risen and fallen in remarkably close step and further proves the link between the two.

1987
The most violent storm recorded since 1703 sweeps through southern England, uprooting more than 15 million trees.

1988
The UN asks for a high-level scientific assessment of climate change, which leads to the establishment of the Intergovernmental Panel on Climate Change (IPCC). Its role is to produce regular, detailed reports on the conclusions of climate scientists worldwide. The first report appears in 1990.

1990
A tropical cyclone (hurricane) in the Indian Ocean creates a storm surge 20 ft (6 m) high that sweeps up the Bay of Bengal and floods parts of the low-lying Bangladesh, causing around 148,000 deaths.

Ice cores at Vostok prove that atmospheric carbon dioxide levels affect global temperature

1990
US geophysicist Syukuro Manabe (below) uses a computer model of world climate to show that global warming could weaken the Gulf Stream, possibly making northern Europe cooler rather than warmer.

Torrential rain causes heavy flooding in Britain in 2000

1991
The eruption of Mount Pinatubo in the Philippines ejects a dust cloud into the atmosphere, making average global temperatures drop for two years.

1991–92
Africa suffers its worst dry spell of the 20th century when 2.6 million sq miles (6.7 million sq km) are affected by drought.

1997
Wildfires in Indonesia destroy more than 1,160 sq miles (3,000 sq km) of forest, creating a vast cloud of pollution that adds as much carbon dioxide to the atmosphere as 30–40 percent of the world's fossil fuel consumption.

1997
At a meeting in Kyoto, Japan, representatives of many countries agree to aim for a five percent cut in global greenhouse gas emissions by 2012. The United States and Australia refuse to agree, but it becomes international law in 2005.

1998
Global temperatures are the highest ever recorded.

2000
Torrential rain and flooding hit Britain during the wettest fall recorded in 300 years.

2001
The IPCC produces its third report, which shows that there is no longer any doubt among climate scientists that human activity is causing global climate change. The report includes the "hockey stick" graph showing temperatures over the past 1,000 years, and the sharp upturn in the 20th century.

2002
The Larsen-B ice shelf near the tip of the Antarctic Peninsula disintegrates within 35 days, and 1,254 sq miles (3,250 sq km) of ice drift away to melt in the ocean.

US geophysicist Syukuro Manabe and his computer projections

2003
Europe experiences its most extreme heatwave for at least 500 years with temperatures over 104°F (40°C), and at least 30,000 people die as a result.

2004
A study published in the scientific journal *Nature* concludes that up to 52 percent of plant and animal species could face extinction because of climate change by the year 2050.

2004
Measurements of ocean currents associated with the Gulf Stream indicate that the flow has slowed since the 1960s. They suggest that the Gulf Stream might be under threat.

2004–5
A warm, snow-free winter forces most of the ski resorts in Washington and Oregon to shut down midway through the season.

2005
Australia records its warmest year since reliable temperature observations became available in 1910. The previous record was set in 1998.

2005
The British Antarctic Survey reveals that the massive West Antarctic ice sheet could be disintegrating—an event that could raise world sea levels by up to 16 ft (5 m).

2005
The Atlantic suffers the worst hurricane season on record, with 14 named storms. One of these, Hurricane Katrina, destroys much of New Orleans, Louisiana.

2005
US climate scientist James Hansen warns that, unless the amount of carbon dioxide in the atmosphere is stabilized, Earth will soon be warmer than it has been in a million years. Stabilization is possible, but it will involve reducing emissions by 60 to 80 percent.

A snow-free winter in Washington closes the ski resorts in 2004

2005
Global temperatures match the 1998 record.

2006
Several of Greenland's glaciers are reported to be flowing much faster than in the past, indicating that the fringes of the Greenland ice sheet are reacting to global warming more quickly than had been predicted.

2007
The IPCC produces its fourth report, which predicts that if no measures are taken to limit greenhouse gas emissions, and there is rapid economic growth, average global temperatures could increase by 7.2°F (4°C) by 2100.

2007
China takes over from the United States as the world's biggest producer of greenhouse gases, even though China's emissions per person are only a quarter of those in the US. Much of the rise is caused by increased electricity generation by coal-fired power plants.

2007
Severe heatwaves hit southern Europe, with temperatures peaking at 114.8°F (46°C) in Greece, causing wildfires and deaths from heatstroke. Meanwhile torrential rain strikes Britain, causing serious flooding. The intensity of the rainfall matches computer models of the changing climate.

2007
James Hansen and five other scientists warn that Earth is getting close to severe climate changes that could threaten civilization itself.

Find out more

Every day there are items in the newspapers and other media about the latest scientific research into climate change. More detailed information about this work can be found on websites, in museums, and at institutions that specialize in this area. You can also find out more by doing some research of your own. Take daily records of the weather, or work out how much energy you could save as a family by changing your way of life.

USEFUL WEBSITES

• These five sites all offer good overviews of global warming and ways of tackling it, with useful links:
www.eo.ucar.edu/kids/index.html
http://tiki.oneworld.net/global_warming/climate_home.html
www.epa.gov/climatechange/kids/
www.coolkidsforacoolclimate.com/
www.pewclimate.org/global-warming-basics/kidspage.cfm
• The British Antarctic Survey shows life in the field:
www.antarctica.ac.uk
• This next site, run by the US Department of Energy, is all about fossil fuels:
www.fe.doe.gov/education/energylessons/index.html
• The US University Corporation for Atmospheric Research (UCAR) has a useful website covering the basics of weather and climate:
www.eo.ucar.edu/basics/index.html
• NASA has an excellent website giving information about climate change:
http://earthobservatory.nasa.gov/Library/GlobalWarmingUpdate/
• The respected UK magazine *New Scientist* has an extensive online report about climate change that is easy to read:
http://environment.newscientist.com/channel/earth/climate-change
• The Real Climate website is a blog run by an international team of top climate scientists:
www.realclimate.org/

Museum trips
Many science and natural history museums have excellent exhibits covering topics raised in this book. They include Harvard University Center for the Environment in the Geological Museum, the Natural World Museum in San Francisco, and London's Science Museum and Natural History Museum.

Visits and virtual visits
Your school may be able to arrange a visit to a wind farm (right), hydroelectric station, a tidal barrage, recycling plant, a zero-emissions housing development, an eco-city, or local wildlife reserve. The British Antarctic Survey provides photographic updates daily and the Survey currently has webcams (below) at Halley and Rothera stations as well as on board RRS *James Clark Ross* and RRS *Ernest Shackleton*. There is also a webcam at King Edward Point run by the Government of South Georgia.

What's your effect?
With online help, you can work out what kind of impact you are having on the climate and how you can minimize it. Calculate your "carbon footprint" with these two websites:
www.bestfootforward.com/ and www.climatecrisis.net
You'll also find great ideas on how to lessen your impact at these two sites: www.energysavingtrust.org.uk/ and www.ase.org/section/_audience/consumers/kids
Finally, if you'd like to use your computer to help model future climates, try downloading a climate model from here:
http://climateprediction.net/

Glossary

Parched earth during a drought

ABSORPTION
The process of sucking in or absorbing something. Usually a liquid is sucked into a solid, such as water being absorbed by the ground.

ALBEDO
Every object reflects light. The albedo of an object is the extent or level to which it reflects light.

ALKALINE
Describing a substance that contains particular minerals which make it opposite to acidic.

ANTHRACITE
This is a very hard form of coal. It has the highest carbon count of all the different coal types and contains the fewest impurities.

ATMOSPHERE
The layers of gases surrounding Earth or any other planet.

BACTERIA
A large group of microscopic single-celled organisms, probably best known for causing disease, but also important for helping decomposition and recycling of substances.

BIOFUEL
Fuel made from biomass, usually plants. If used on a small scale, it can be better for the environment than using fossil fuels.

BIOMASS
Material made from living organisms, such as plants and animals and their byproducts, such as manure or garden waste.

BIOSPHERE
The part of Earth's surface and atmosphere that is inhabited by living things.

CARBOHYDRATE
Any of a large group of organic compounds, such as sugars and starches, that contain carbon, hydrogen, and oxygen. It is a source of food for animals. For example, potatoes and bread contain carbohydrate.

CARBON
A non-metallic element that occurs in all organic compounds.

Biofuel

CARBONATE
A salt made from carbonic acid.

CARBON DIOXIDE
A colorless, odorless gas formed when carbon combines with oxygen. It is breathed out by animals and used by plants for photosynthesis. It is the main greenhouse gas responsible for global warming.

CARBON EMISSIONS
The carbon dioxide released, or emitted, into the atmosphere. Most of these emissions come from burning fossil fuels.

CARBON FOOTPRINT
Every person is responsible for the emission of a certain amount of carbon-based greenhouse gas, either by power stations that burn fossil fuels to generate electricity, or by transportation that uses oil-based fuels. This is called their carbon footprint. The more electricity or fuel used, the bigger the carbon footprint.

COPPICING
A sustainable method of harvesting firewood from trees that preserves the tree and enables it to grow more branches.

DATA
A series of observations, measurements, or facts, used to help draw conclusions or back up research.

DROUGHT
A long period of time with no rainfall.

EVAPORATE
To change from a liquid form to a gaseous one. Water evaporates into water vapor.

FEEDBACK
A reaction in response to a particular event.

FERTILE
Describing land with plenty of nutrients that enable plants to grow well.

FLUCTUATIONS
Irregular changes or variations of level or flow rate, as in temperatures, sea levels, or ocean currents.

FOSSIL FUELS
Carbon or hydrocarbon-based fuels—such as coal, oil, and natural gas—formed by the partial preservation of plant and animal remains. When burned, they release carbon dioxide.

FUEL CELL
An electrochemical energy converter. It produces electricity from outside supplies of fuel such as hydrogen. Fuel cells can operate virtually continuously as long as the supply of fuel stays constant.

GEOLOGY
The scientific study of the rocks and structure of planet Earth.

GLACIER
A slowly moving mass of ice formed originally from thick snow.

HYDROCARBON
An organic compound consisting entirely of hydrogen and carbon.

ICE SHELF
A thick floating platform of ice that forms where an ice sheet or glacier flows down to a coastline and onto the ocean surface.

INDUSTRIALIZATION
The development of industry, such as manufacturing or construction, on a huge scale. Industry at this level relies on the creation of a huge amount of energy, usually by burning fossil fuels.

INFRARED
A form of radiation detectable as heat, which has a wavelength longer than visible light but shorter than that of radio waves.

Gasoline pump (see FOSSIL FUELS)

INSULATION
Materials or techniques used to reduce the rate at which heat is conducted, for example through the walls of a building.

INTERACT
Two or more things acting in such a way that they influence one another.

MIGRATION
Traveling from one area or country to another. Many animals, especially birds, migrate from one continent to another.

Glacier

MOLECULE
A group of atoms held together by chemical bonds. For example, a molecule of methane (natural gas) is made up of one carbon atom bonded to four hydrogen atoms.

MONSOON
A seasonal change of wind that affects the weather, especially in tropical regions where it causes wet and dry seasons.

OXIDIZE
To have a chemical reaction with the gas oxygen. When carbon reacts with oxygen, it oxidizes and turns to carbon dioxide.

OXYGEN
A colorless, odorless gas, essential for the life of most organisms. It makes up about one fifth of the air in Earth's atmosphere.

OZONE
A form of oxygen. The ozone layer helps block harmful radiation from the Sun.

PARTICLE
A minute bit of matter.

PERMAFROST
Ground that is permanently frozen.

PHOTOSYNTHESIS
The process by which plants and similar organisms use sunlight to make carbohydrate food from water and carbon dioxide..

PLANKTON
Tiny living things that drift in the upper, sunlit layer of oceans and lakes. They include plant-like organisms and animals.

Monsoon rain

POLLUTION
Contamination with either harmful or poisonous substances.

PROJECTION
A prediction based on known evidence and observations. Scientists gather data which allows them to make projections.

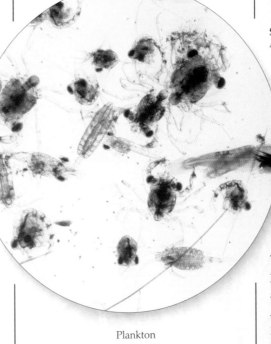
Plankton

RADIOACTIVE
Describing an atomic nucleus that automatically sends out waves of energy in the form of electromagnetic waves. The element uranium is naturally radioactive.

REFRIGERANT
A fluid that is used to absorb heat and pump it out of refrigerators and freezers. In the past the most common refrigerants were compounds called chlorofluorocarbons (CFCs)—these are powerful greenhouse gases that also destroy protective ozone in the atmosphere.

SEA LEVEL
The level of the sea surface in comparison to the land. All heights on land are measured in relation to average sea level.

SENSORS
Anything, such as a microphone, that receives a signal and responds to it. Scientists use sensors to help them gather data.

SOLAR POWER
Energy produced from devices called solar panels and solar collectors, which use sunlight to generate heat or electricity.

SOLAR RADIATION
The waves of light produced by the Sun. Some of this energy is visible as sunlight.

Tropical rainforest

STORM SURGE
A local rise in sea level water caused by a low-pressure weather system, such as a hurricane or tropical cyclone.

TEMPERATE
A climate that is neither tropical nor polar. Generally it is mild in temperature with some rainfall.

TROPICAL
A climate that is very hot and often very wet, or humid.

TUNDRA
The cold, treeless, largely barren land that fringes the polar regions, between the forests and the permanent ice.

TURBINE
A machine that converts the movement of air or water into mechanical energy by using it to turn a bladed rotor.

VEGETATION
Plant life as a whole, especially the plant life of a particular region.

WATER VAPOR
The invisible, gaseous form of water, which forms part of the atmosphere.

Index

AB

acidification, oceans, 34, 42
aerosols, 19, 25
air pollution, 19, 24, 25
air travel, 23, 61, 62, 63, 65
albedo effect, 12
animals: carbon cycle, 10
  evolution, 34
  extinctions, 34, 35, 41
  methane emissions, 24, 62, 64
Antarctica, 16, 28–29, 31
anthracite, 10
Arctic, 17, 28–29, 36–37, 40
Arrhenius, Svante, 7, 66
Atlantic Ocean, 31
atmosphere, 6, 8–9, 17
beef, 24, 62
bicycles, 61, 62
biofuels, 55, 60, 61
birds, 17, 34, 35
BP, 48
buses, 61, 62, 65

C

campaigns, 48
carbon cycle, 10–11, 21
carbon dioxide: absorption in
  oceans, 31, 67
  carbon capture, 51
  carbon cycle, 10–11
  cutting emissions, 48–49
  deforestation and, 18–19
  fossil fuels, 20–21, 65
  greenhouse effect, 8, 9, 64–66
  global warming, 7
  levels in atmosphere, 17
  volcanoes, 11
carbon footprints, 62–65, 69
"carbon-neutral" fuels, 19
carbon offsetting schemes, 63
carbon rationing, 62
carbon trading, 49
carbonic acid, 34
cars, 23, 60, 62, 65, 66
catastrophic changes, 42–43, 48
cattle ranching, 24, 62
cells, atmosphere, 7
cement, 24
chlorofluorocarbons (CFCs), 24,
  25, 64
cities, 49
  eco-cities, 59
  floods, 45
  rainfall, 47

sea level rises, 40, 43
tidal defenses, 46
climate models, 38–39, 67, 69
climate zones, 7
clouds, 12
coal, 7, 10–11, 20–22, 50–51, 65
computers, 23, 38
continental drift, 15
coral, 17, 32, 34, 42
cows 24, 62
currents: atmosphere, 6, 7
  ocean, 6, 31, 32, 33, 54, 68
cyclones, 31, 67

DEF

decay, carbon cycle, 10
deforestation, 18–19, 27
deserts, 6, 14, 27, 40, 44, 47, 66
diseases, 35, 44
droughts, 26, 27, 35, 45, 66–68
Earth: atmosphere, 6–7
  axis drift, 14
  greenhouse effect, 8–9
  natural climate change, 14–15
  orbital cycles, 14
  tilt, 6, 14
electric cars, 60
electricity: dependence on, 22, 23
  energy efficiency, 58–59
  from fossil fuels, 20, 22, 66, 68
  local power plants, 56
  nuclear power, 52
  reducing carbon emissions,
  50–51
  renewable sources, 54–55
electronic equipment, 62
energy: electricity generation,
  50–51
  energy efficiency, 58–59
  nuclear power, 52–53
  renewable sources, 54–55
  technological revolution, 16–17
evolution, 34, 35
extinctions, 12, 34, 41, 42, 43, 66,
  68
famines, 27, 66, 67
farming, 24, 26, 27, 45, 47, 55, 64,
  66
feedbacks, 12–13, 14, 28
fires, 18–19, 27, 42
fish, 34, 36, 42
floods, 30, 31, 40–41, 44–45,
  46–47
food, 23, 45, 62, 63
food chains, 36
forests, 18–19, 27, 42, 49
fossil fuels, 20–21, 22, 48, 50–51,
  64, 65
fossils, 14
freezing temperatures 9

GHI

Gaia theory, 13
garbage, 24, 65
gas, natural, 20, 21, 50, 51, 65
gases, greenhouse, 8, 18, 64, 68
gasification, coal, 51
geothermal energy, 55
glaciers, 28–29, 30, 40, 45, 68
"Global Climate Coalition," 48
Gore, Al, 48
greenhouse effect, 8–9
greenhouse gases, 8, 18, 64, 68
heat pumps, 57
heating, 22, 55, 56, 59, 62
heatwaves, 26, 40, 67, 68
houses, 59
hurricanes, 31, 41, 44, 45
hybrid cars, 60
hydroelectric power, 54, 57
hydrogen, 61
ice: feedbacks, 12, 28
  ice cores, 16, 67
  melting, 28–30, 36–37, 40
  methane hydrate, 43
  soot pollution, 25
ice ages, 7, 14, 15, 66
ice sheets, 6, 16, 28–9, 40, 43, 67,
  68
icebergs, 28–30, 43
Industrial Revolution, 20, 66
industry, 7, 20, 64
insects, 6, 35
Intergovernmental Panel on
  Climate Change (IPCC), 48,
  67, 68

KLM

Keeling, Charles, 9, 67
Kyoto Protocol, 49, 68
lakes, 26
landfill sites, 24, 63
lighting, 59
lignite, 10
limestone, 11, 24
liquified natural gas (LNG), 51
Little Ice Age, 15, 66
Lovelock, James, 13
meat, 24, 62
meltwater, 30, 40
methane: animal emissions,
  62, 64
  catastrophic changes, 42
  greenhouse effect, 8, 24, 64
  landfill sites, 24
  natural gas, 20
  from ocean floor, 43
  rice growing, 24
methane hydrate, 43
migration, 44

Milankovitch cycles, 14, 66
mining, 20–21, 50, 53
Moon, 9
mountains, 35

NOP

natural gas, 20, 21, 50, 51, 65
nitrous oxide, 8, 24, 25, 64
nuclear power, 52–53
oceans, 6, 9, 28–31
  acidification, 34, 42
  carbon dioxide absorption, 9, 67
  currents, 31, 32, 33, 54
  feedbacks, 12
  methane release, 43
  research, 32–33
  sea level rises, 30, 40, 43, 44,
  45, 46, 68
oil, 7, 20, 21, 48, 51, 65, 66
orbital cycles, Earth, 14
organic decay, 10
ozone, 8
pack ice, 36, 37, 40
peat, 10–11, 19
permafrost, 28, 40, 42
photosynthesis, 10, 11
plages, 14
planets, 6, 9
plankton, 10, 13, 20, 30, 31, 33,
  42, 43
plants, 6
  biofuels, 55
  carbon cycle, 10, 11
  carbon uptake, 13
  evolution, 34
  extinctions, 34, 35, 41
  farming, 26, 27, 45, 47, 55
  fossil fuels, 20
plastics, 22
polar bears, 36–37, 40
pollution, 19, 24, 25, 37
power plants, 22, 50–51, 52–53,
  55, 56, 64
predicting future climates, 38–39

RS

radioactivity, 52, 53
railroads, 7, 23, 52, 61, 62, 63
rainfall, 27, 31, 40
rainforests, 6, 42, 61, 62
recycling, 60, 63
refugees, 44
renewable energy, 54–55
research, 32–33
respiration, 10, 11
rice, 24, 47
rivers, 27, 47, 54
rocks, 11, 14, 20

sea level rises, 30, 40, 43, 44, 45,
  46, 68
seasons, 6, 14
shopping, 63
smoke, forest fires, 19
snow, 7, 12, 25
solar energy, 8, 10, 12, 14, 54, 55,
  56, 58
soot, 19, 25, 51
storms, 30, 31, 40, 41, 46, 47,
  66–68
sugar, 10
sulfuric acid, 15
Sun, 6, 8, 11, 53
sunspots, 14

TUVW

technology, 16, 48, 60
temperatures: atmosphere and,
  6, 9
  catastrophic changes, 43, 48
  climate zones, 7
  feedbacks, 12–13, 14
  heatwaves, 26, 40
  human factors, 16–17
  natural climate change, 14–15
  predicting future climates,
  38–39
  rise in, 7, 68
  tipping points, 13
tidal barrages, energy
  generation, 54
tidal defenses, 46
tipping points, 13
transportation, 23, 49, 60–61, 62,
  64, 65
trains, 61, 65
trees, 17, 18–19, 35, 41, 42, 49, 63
tundra, 42
United Nations, 48
uranium, 52, 53
Venus, 9
volcanoes, 7, 9, 11, 15, 43, 54, 55,
  66, 68
water, 6, 7
  droughts, 26, 27, 35, 45, 66–68
  renewable energy, 54–55, 57
  shortages, 45
water vapor, 8, 12
watermills, 54
wave energy, 54
weather, 6, 7
websites, 69
wetlands, 35
wildfires, 27, 42, 68
wildlife reserves, 46
wind power, 54, 55, 57, 58
winds, 7
wood, 18–19, 20, 56

Acknowledgments

Dorling Kindersley would like to thank:
Stewart J. Wild for proof-reading; Rebecca Painter & Kate Scarborough for pp64–71; Hilary Bird for the index; David Ekholm-Jálbum, Sunita Gahir, Susan St. Louis, Kate Scarborough, Lisa Stock, & Bulent Yusuf for the clip art; Kate Scarborough & Jim Green for the wall chart; Jenny Siklos for Americanization.

The publisher thanks the following for their kind permission to reproduce their photographs:
(a=above b=below/bottom c=center l=left r=right t=top) **Alamy Images:** Sotheby's 15br; **Alamy Images:** Alaska Stock LLC 43tr; Arco Images 61tl; Simon Belcher 59tl; Mark Boulton 56t, 58c; James Cheadle 2c, 22-23b; Gary Cook 41cl; Dennis Cox 60-61bl; Elvele Images 36br; Pavel Filatov 42t; Clynt Garnham 57tl; David Kilpatrick 69tl; Robert McGouey 51cr; Renee Morris 35b; Motoring Picture Library 60cl; Edward Parker 49tr; paul-hill.co.uk 61b; Sergio Pitamitz 12t; Rainer Raffalski 49b; Vera Schimetzek 47c; Andy Sutton 47tl; VIEW Pictures Ltd 59b; **Arup:** 58-59b; **British Antarctic Survey:** 69b; **Bryan and Cherry Alexander Photography:** 28bl, 30cl, 36c; **Courtesy of Climateprediction.net:** 39b; **Corbis:** Steve Austin 17c; Bettmann 21b; William Campbell /

Sygma 44c; Stephane Cardinale / People Avenue 48tr; Ashley Cooper 30t; Howard Davies 49c; Philip de Bay / Historical Picture Archive 44t; Dominique Derda / France 2 44b; Dewitt Jones 35c; Viktor Korotayev / Reuters 21c; John Madere 62t; Gideon Mendel 47b; Sally A. Morgan / Ecoscene 18c; Guang Niu / Reuters 24l, 27l; Douglas Peebles 46r; Rickey Rogers / Reuters 27tr; Gilles Sabrié 25c; Skyscan 52cr; Jim Sugar 9bl, 68b; Alison Wright 56-57b; **DK Images:** Courtesy of the National Maritime Museum, London 51br; Katie Williamson 71l; Katy Williamson 1b; Jerry Young 70t; **Ecoscene:** Peter Dannatt 53cl; Stuart Donachie 32t; **Energy Saving Trust:** Simon Punter 57c; **Environmentalists for Nuclear Energy:** 13cl; **ESA:** Envisat 33tr; **FLPA:** Nigel Cattlin 25tl; Larry West 41c; Konrad Wothe 37t; **Getty Images:** Fred Bavendam 34t; The Bridgeman Art Library 29bl; Peter Cade 62-63b; Chien-min Chung 50r; Michal Cizek / AFP 26cl; Adrian Dennis 48tl; Peter Essick / Aurora 68r; Stephen Ferry 18-19c; Michael & Patricia Fogden 34-35c; Tim Graham 55tr; Satoru Imai / Sebun Photo 54t; Saeed Khan / AFP 48b; John Lamb 62tr; Alex Livesey / Logan Mock-Bunting 42b; Mark Moffett 18l; Bruno Morandi 40-41b; Stuart O'Sullivan 58t; Tyler Stableford 12c; Teubner 55cr; Toru Yamanaka / AFP

49tl; **Global Warming Art (www.globalwarmingart.com):** 39tr; **International Panel on Climate Change:** 39t; **Marine Current Turbines TM Ltd:** 54-55; **NASA Goddard Space Flight Center:** 26bl, 26br; **National Geographic Image Collection:** James P. Blair 18b; Ralph Lee Hopkins 36t; **Courtesy of the Natural Environment Research Council:** 32-33b; **Courtesy of NOAA:** GFDL 38-39b, 40t; **PA Photos:** Charles Rex Arbogast / AP Photo 26cr; Vinai Dithajohn / AP 19t; Dado Galdieri / AP 43c; Kent Gilbert / AP 46l; Nati Harnik / AP 20-21; Itsuo Inouye / AP 38t; Stephen Kelly / PA Archive 48cl; Bullit Marquez 15l; John Mcconnico / AP 28cl; John D. Mchugh / AP 41t; Martin Meissner / Ap 50-51; Leslie Neuhaus / AP 27c; David J. Phillip / AP 45b; Aijaz Rahi / AP 31br; Solar Systems / AP 55cl; USGS / AP 43l; Liu Yingyi / AP 23tl; **PunchStock:** Purestock 57tr; **Reuters:** Action Images 31bl; Mario Anzuoni 27br; Jayanta Shaw 44-45b; **Rex Features:** Dennis Gilbert / View Pictures 59tr; SplashdownDirect / Michael Nolan 37l; Sipa Press 29ca, 29t, 53cr, 53t; **Science Photo Library:** 9br; Steve Allen 52br; Martin Bond 22bl; British Antarctic Survey 7t, 16-17b; John Clegg 20c; Tony Craddock 43br; Bernhard Edmaier 10b, 28br; Mauro Fermariello 17tl, 17tr; Richard Folwell 21tr; Simon Fraser 24-25; Brian Gadsby 9tl; Geospace 3, 16t; GSFC / NASA 26tl; Tony Hertz / Agstockusa 24t; Ian Hooton 40cl; Institute Of Oceanographic Sciences 32c; David Hay Jones 13cr; Ted Kinsman 13t, 59tc; Dr Ken Macdonald 33tl;

Munoz-Yague / Eurelios 67b; NASA 19c; NASA / Goddard Space Flight Center 29bc; Bjorn Svensson 55br; Take 27 Ltd 42-43b; TRL Ltd 52bl; **Still Pictures:** Joerg Boethling 47tr; Paul Glendell 68t; Godard / Andia.fr 54bl; Marilyn Kazmers 32b; Mark Lynas 30b; Hartmut Schwarzbach / argus 61tr; **Courtesy of US Navy:** JOC(SW/AW) David Rush 33cr

Illustration: Ed Merritt 28–29 maps; Peter Winfield 8cb, 12–13b, 14br, 17br, 25br, 38cl, 39tl, 48br, 51tr, cl, 57 br, 60 tr, 64–64

Wall chart: Alamy Images: James Cheadle clb (plane); Motoring Picture Library crb (car); DK Images: Rowan Greenwood ca; Natural History Museum, London tl (plants); Marine Current Turbines TM Ltd.: crb (marine currents); PA Photos: Anthony Mitchell / AP ftr; Science Photo Library: Simon Fraser / Northumbrian Environmental Management Ltd. bl; Geospace c

Jacket: *Front:* Alamy Images: Vick Fisher (b); Barrie Harwood (ftr); Edward Parker (tr). Getty Images: Panoramic Images (tc); Jim Reed/Digital Vision (ftl). Science Photo Library: G. Brad Lewis (tl). *Back:* Alamy Images: Mike Lane (br); Doug Wilson (bl). Corbis: Lester Lefkowitz (cr). Getty Images: Panoramic Images (cb). Science Photo Library: British Antarctic Survey (cla); NASA (ca); R.B. Husar/NASA (tr).

All other images © Dorling Kindersley
For further information see: **www.dkimages.com**